BLOODY BOOTS

VTRATA

PEYTON JAMES ROBINSON

Edited by
JESSE RAY DILL

PJR- For my Dad

JRD- For my Grandma

PROLOGUE

The world calls me a hero, I look in the mirror and see a villain. Truthfully, the only difference between the two is who you want to save, and the measures you're willing to take to do so. Besides that, they're pretty much the same- just a person trying to do the "right" thing. I come from a family of good natured people. The word around my town is, 'Those Robinsons are loud and energetic, but they got moral fiber.'

In my family, we are all taught the same lesson, 'You do the right thing, no matter the cost.' It's a lesson my father taught me, and his father taught him. I used to believe I knew what the right thing to do was, but now I'm not so sure. I'm not even sure what qualifies as a good person anymore. War has a way of blurring those lines between good and evil.

My mother's side is a different story. Everyone on my mother's side is extremely emotional, crazy, and loves hard. When people ask me, 'Peyton, how did you do that?' I laugh and say,

"The high morals from my father's side, mixed with the craziness from my mother's side, made one hell of a combination." I also think it stems from where I live. I grew up in Tennessee, the Volunteer State. We got our nickname because we're always willing to lend a helping hand. Southern hospitality is a real thing. It probably comes from Tennessee being the frontier, but I think it also has a lot to do with our own religious beliefs. In my hometown, there are more churches than restaurants. In church they told us,

"Jesus ate with sinners. Jesus helped people that nobody believed was worth anything. Jesus gave his life for humankind. Be like Jesus." Everyone needs a hero to look up to. I don't really consider myself a religious man, but Jesus is someone I aspire to be like.

1

A FATAL PROMISE

"I used to think my life was hell until I walked into it. I've experienced a lot of pain throughout my years, and it's scary to think that I'm still in my early twenties. Every time I thought it was over, I found that I wasn't even halfway through. At the time, I believed that reality was hell, and that it was my responsibility to make it better. The truth is, reality is what you make of it, because your worst day is someone else's best. **Life can either be a blessing or a curse, and you decide which one it is."** -Peyton Robinson

I'd be lying if I said this all started when the war began, it was actually a few weeks prior. I came home from work to see Midnight, my pet guinea pig, not moving. I felt him, and knew he was alive, but didn't have long. I'd seen guinea pigs die before. They expand, and their body temperature goes down while slipping into a near-comatose state. There wasn't much I could do but wait until morning.

I stayed with him all night, trying to feed him anything with water. He tried nibbling on a celery stick, but stopped after a few bites. He never had a problem eating, he'd eat his weight in food if I let him. I brought him to the vet in a shoe box the following day. I went inside, tears flowing down my face, begging for a doctor. The woman working the desk just shook her head then said,

"I'm sorry Mr. Robinson. Dr. Smith doesn't work the weekends. He's gonna have to survive till tomorrow." I bowed my head and walked towards the door, but not before she added, "He's really cute." All I could think was, *Emotional support won't do anything.* I went home, and my roommates, Jackson and Aaron, called out of work to stay with him. Several friends came over to see him, since we knew his time was ending. Once 9 o'clock came, I asked everyone to leave so it would just be us.

I stayed up with him all night, telling him how much I loved him, and feeling guilty about not being the owner he deserved. He was the sweetest creature to ever exist. I'd throw 'Pig Parties,' and dozens of people would come to play with him. Whenever I had a bad day, he cheered me up. He knew what I was feeling, so he'd press up against the cage for me to hold him. He was the best brother a guy could ask for. Eventually, I passed out, then woke up minutes later with him missing from my arms. I frantically searched my bed, but when I found him, he was barely alive. As his life slipped away, I held him close, and told him my final goodbyes.

"I wanted you to see me become a man. I wanted to build you a sanctuary so you could run around free! Not be trapped in this apartment like a prisoner. I wanted you to see me succeed," as I felt his heart grow weaker, I made him a promise, "I'll do it, Midnight. I'll do it. I'll give my life to humanity. I won't stop until I save it. Your death won't be in vain. I love you." He licked my hand, and then his heart stopped, and he was gone. He held on long enough for me to wake up before passing away. I felt something die inside me.

I know what you're thinking, 'It's just a guinea pig.' But if it was a dog you'd understand? The next day, my roommates Aaron and Jackson helped me bury him on my dad's property, then we said our goodbyes. They went to the car, while I hovered over the rock we made to be his gravestone and said,

"This world took you from me. Because of their ignorance. Because they didn't think you mattered. Because you were just a rodent. You weren't just a rodent. You were my best friend. You saved me from ending my life so many times, and you were always there, happy to see me when I came home. Because of ignorance, you died. Because of ignorance, humanity will always be trapped. Cursed to follow this endless cycle. Well, I'm going to break it. I, Peyton Robinson, will save humanity. I'm going to rid this world of ignorance, even if it comes at the cost of my life. I promise." I'm not perfect, I've failed countless times, but I wouldn't go back on my word unless through death.

2

CALL TO ACTION

I'll never forget that day. February 24, 2022. The day my life changed forever. It was a Thursday, so it meant my early morning introduction to American politics class. After class, I walked home, jamming to my music. It had been a rough two weeks without Midnight, but I knew that no matter what, I had to keep moving forward. I walked in to find Aaron and Jackson glued to the TV screen.

"Peyton, Russia invaded Ukraine!" Jackson declared as soon as I walked in. I was in shock. We'd known about Putin placing troops on Ukraine's border, but didn't think he actually had the nerve to invade. The three of us sat on the edge of the couch waiting eagerly as more news came flooding in by the hour. We, like most Americans, thought World War 3 was nearing. After some thought, I went to get us food, then we spent the rest of the night watching the news, waiting for war to be declared.

"There is no way we're going to stand by and let Putin do this!" I declared to them, "Ukraine is a democracy. We're America! We have to stop him!" I was confident that we would stand up for democracy and I was ready for it. That night, we stayed up and spent what we thought was our last night alive together—joking about the 3rd Great War. We've always said we would fight in the war when it came, but we didn't think it would arrive so quickly. We were all scared, but none of us would admit it. All I wanted to do was ensure they wouldn't be afraid anymore.

The next day, I went to the army recruitment office and got my papers. I took my forms home, filled them out, then waited for the declaration of war. I was told quite often that my decision to go was an impulsive one. I need to clarify that it was far from it. From the moment the war started, I was ready to fight. I was prepared to lay my life down and accept the consequences. Don't tell me something about me, when you're not me.

Days went by before we received news about America's next move. President Biden issued sanctions against Russia then gave Ukraine billions of dollars. I was outraged. *What will a couple of billion dollars do against one of the most powerful countries in the world?* I thought as we watched the news, *It takes hands. It takes people. Not just money.* I knew that my military papers were a waste, so I just threw them in the trash. It was time for plan B- join the Ukrainian Legion. The Ukrainian Legion is a volunteer force composed of people worldwide willing to fight the Russians. There were a few requirements, all that I understand and respect, but still disagree with,

1. Be 25 years of age.
2. Have previous military experience.
3. Be in good physical shape.

I didn't have any of these, but it was worth a shot. I submitted my application then called the Ukrainian Legion. After a few days of waiting, I looked at my application and saw that it had been denied. I called them, thinking my commitment would change their mind. They said what I feared,

"Sorry. You don't qualify." Those few words made my whole world crumble. Feeling defeated, I slumped down in my gaming chair and sighed. I was stuck. I knew it was my destiny to go, but it seemed impossible. I knew this was what God was calling me to do, but it wasn't just for him, I wanted it too. I remember watching the news one day with my roommates. They played a video of a bomb exploding in a Ukrainian home, with a little girl screaming out in terror. I was so upset that I had to excuse myself to my room to cry. I wanted to help them, I wanted to save them. It was tearing me apart knowing innocent people were dying, while all I was doing was standing still.

At night, I'd have nightmares of the war. One night, I dreamed of a little girl in a Ukrainian city. She had straight brown hair, piercing blue eyes, and wore a long white dress. She couldn't have been any older than eight. She was running down a long, windy road in a subdivision. The city was on fire, and citizens were running in each direction. I followed after her. It led to a brick wall, and she frantically tried to scale it as Russian soldiers came into view. I tried to run towards her to help, but my legs wouldn't budge. They seemed to be glued to the road. She screamed out for help as the Russians moved closer. All the while, I stood still. She screamed out in terror, and it made me wake up screaming in a cold sweat. I looked around my room. My head stiffened when I saw my gaming chair. In it sat the girl from my dream.

At first, I didn't believe it. I closed my eyes and went back to sleep. I dreamt the same nightmare and woke up screaming again. When I woke again, I looked towards my chair to find her still there. I smoked a lot of weed in college, even hallucinated, but I was definitely sober that morning. I leaped out of bed and moved closer to her.

"What the hell?" I said to the girl. She stared back at me aimlessly as I approached her. Once my hand was inches from her face, she whispered,

"Help." It was as quiet as a mouse, but it sounded like thunder in my ears. I closed my eyes and wished her away. When I opened my eyes, she was gone. I went back to bed, then glanced back at the chair to find her there again. I walked into my kitchen to find my roommates sitting on the couch. I asked them to come into my room.

"Do you see anything?" I asked Aaron and Jackson. They looked around my room and gave me an 'Are you okay?' look. I pointed to my chair, and they stared at it, confused.

"What's wrong with it?" Jackson asked. The girl stared blankly at them.

"The girl right there." I pointed at the chair. Aaron went to sit in the chair, and right before he sat, the girl slipped out of the chair and onto the floor. She made a loud 'oof' sound, then moved to the futon beside my bed. I turned back to Aaron and Jackson, who looked at me confused. I asked them if they saw it, but they shook their heads no. After being told I was crazy, they left my room. I shut the door then marched over to her.

"What do you want?" I yelled. She looked up at me with her piercing blue eyes then replied softly,

"Help." Her eyes looked clouded, as if she was in a trance.

"I can't help you. I'm useless. I'm a stupid, lazy, stoner college kid. How do you expect me to help you?" The girl stared blankly at me, and I began to ignore her. I hoped that if I did, then she would go away. She did not, however. She followed me everywhere I went. She was there on my walk to school, in the chair next to me in class, in the passenger seat of my car. Every time I fell asleep, I'd see her sitting in my chair then wake to see her still there. A few days later, I was in my kitchen making breakfast. As I was smearing peanut butter onto my toast, she hummed a tune to herself. I couldn't take it anymore. I turned to her then yelled,

"I can't help you, so just leave me alone!" She looked up at me, and I saw the cloudiness in her eyes fade. She started to cry. She crashed onto the floor and began to wail uncontrollably. I felt even more guilty. At the end of the day, she was still just a child. In a rush, I found a pink stuffed rabbit plushie from my closet then lowered myself to her level.

"I'm sorry. I didn't mean to yell at you. It's okay, look. It's a rabbit. See?" She took the rabbit from my hand then went silent, "You know, I won that rabbit at the fair a few years ago, but I've never done anything with it. How about you hold onto it?" She nodded, then squeezed the rabbit.

"Okay." She sheepishly replied, then we awkwardly looked at each other. I'd never been good at talking with children. You'd think I'd be good with how childish I am.

"I never bothered to ask your name. Can you tell me?"

"Renova, but everyone just calls me Ren." She whispered while holding the rabbit tighter.

"That's a pretty name. My names Peyton. Peyton Robinson. You know, I never gave it a name. Everyone deserves a name. What do you want to name it?" Ren looked down at the rabbit, sniffled, then said,

"Ruby." I knit my eyebrows while smirking,

"Ruby? As in, Max and Ruby the cartoon?" Her face lit up then she quickly nodded her head. It made me let out a light chuckle, "Wow. I didn't know kids these days watched it. Thanks Ren, you just made me not feel like an old bag of dust." I said in an old man's voice, and she let out a light giggle. I remembered what I was going to tell her,

"Listen, Ren, I don't know how to help you. I want to, but there's nothing I can do. I'm sorry." The cloudiness returned to her eyes, then she walked to my chair. She sat and stared at me, Ruby in hand, waiting for what I'd do next.

I continued to live my life, but it wasn't the same. Ren followed me everywhere I went, and I was constantly depressed. I couldn't stop thinking about what the Russians would do if they found her, what the Russians were doing right now. War, to me, is like watching a crime being committed, but it's just thousands of miles away. There was something I could do to help, but I didn't know how. I stopped trying in school, and I quit my job. I had no desire to do anything anymore. All I could do was lay in bed and stare at the ceiling, hoping for an answer.

Then one day it came. I was lying in bed till noon; the energy to do anything was gone. I stared at Ren as she looked back with Ruby in hand. Her eyes screamed at me to save her, but I was standing still. I leaned against my headboard while cradling my face in my hands.

"I don't know how to help you. I'm useless. I'm supposed to be this hero for humanity, but I can't do anything. I'm supposed to be the future President, the protector of the Free world, and I can't even find a way to save one little girl." I couldn't take it anymore. I began to cry. I couldn't keep living if I wasn't helping them. My heart couldn't take it. I scrolled through Snapchat and found a story about a British soldier who was going to Ukraine. The reporter interviewing him asked,

"How are you going to get there? What's your plan? Why even risk your life for this?" The soldier shrugged his shoulders then replied,

"I'm just gonna go over there. It's that simple. I'm doing it because it's the right thing to do, and that's all you need." His words seemed to shake my room like an earthquake. There was something I could do. The answer was there all along, but I refused to see it. I leaped out of bed, took a deep breath, then recalled the two words that define our humanity, *Screw it*. I charged into my kitchen to find my roommates making lunch. I yelled,

"Guys, I have a stupid idea and need y'all to talk me out of it. But you can't." For an hour, we argued back and forth, but they couldn't change my mind.

"Peyton, you can't go over there. You have no combat experience. You're an American in enemy territory. If they find you, they get a promotion! You have no experience in this; you can't do anything." Jackson argued. As valid as his reasoning was, mine was arguably better.

"There is something I can do. I can get on a plane and go over there and do something. I CAN do something! Whether it's handing out food, loading a truck, pulling an injured soldier from the battlefield, or even just being there when they attack. There could be a little girl waiting for me to come save her, and I never do. I can do something! I'm not useless... I'm not worthless. I may die, but it doesn't matter because I'll die here anyway. I can't live with the guilt of knowing I could have done something. Maybe me just being there causes a chain reaction in our favor. There's a chance that I could save someone. It might be a 1 in a million chance, but there's a chance, and I can't live with that. I either die here a coward, or I possibly die there a man. I don't have a choice." It was Aaron's turn to chime in.

"They're not even Americans. They're not our problem. They wouldn't do the same if the roles were reversed." Like lightning, my anger struck.

"If they were Americans you'd understand, but because they're Ukrainians you don't? It doesn't matter what THEY do. It matters what WE do. What would Naruto do? Naruto would go over there and kick Putin's ass! Those people are my responsibility. I am the future President of the United States. That job doesn't start when I take office. That job started the day I was born. You guys know what I believe. If someone wants Freedom, loves democracy, and seeks peace, they are Americans. It doesn't matter what country they're from or what language they speak. They're my people, and I will protect them. They deserve to live like everyone else," I took a deep breath and focused my thoughts, "If you can tell me I'm wrong. Please. I need to be wrong right now. I'm about to take on the entire Russian army single-handed with no military experience. Please tell me I'm wrong. Please!" I begged, but they looked at me stone cold. I went to my room then towards Ren sitting in my chair. I put my hands on her shoulders then said,

"I'm coming to save you. Just wait a little bit longer." Ren smiled then turned away.

3
DEATH CERTIFICATE

I spent the rest of the day planning. It was time for part two of plan B. It was simple- go to Ukraine then ask to join the army in person. I figured if they saw how dedicated I was, they would let some things slide, given it was war. If it fell through, then I'd be on to the next plan. But for now, it was plan B, so I began to prepare. I planned on flying from America to Budapest, Hungary. Then, I would travel north, to a city that borders Ukraine, called Lónya. I chose Lónya because Google Maps showed only a wire fence separating the two countries. There, I would jump the border, and make my way to Kyiv. It was a simple but bold plan.

"Why not just go to Poland?" Jackson asked.

"Because what I'm doing is illegal. They don't want Americans in Ukraine, and someone will try to stop me. But Hungary isn't a part of NATO. They support Russia. It's enemy territory, yes, but I can still go there. All I have to do is not look too suspicious and avoid police officers and the military. If I do get caught, then I'll be thrown in prison for life, but we'll cross that bridge when we get there. One step at a time. Just gotta keep moving forward." Moving forward has been a saying I lived by since I was a kid. I got it from the 'Meet the Robinsons' movie. Since then, no matter what happened, I have kept moving forward.

I also chose Hungary for another reason. During the 1800's, there was a large migration of Jews to Tennessee, one of which was my Great great grandfather John Freed. Freed comes from the Yiddish word, frid, which means peace. Freed became a common middle name in my family, and when you think about it, explains a lot about me. After some research, I found that he originated from Hungary. If I went to Hungary, it could be the first time one of his descendants had been home in almost two-hundred years, so the thought of there being family there made it feel safer. Even though I didn't know who or where they were.

I had to order a passport because I'd never left the country. I got it expedited, and it said it would arrive in 6 weeks. I decided to keep my journey on the down low until then, so the only other people I told were my friends Jesse and Alex. I wanted to ease my friends and family's pain for as long as possible. I was aware of what I would be putting them through, but it seemed like child's play compared to what I was going to experience.

I had six weeks to prepare before my passport arrived. I planned on preparing in week 4, just in case the war ended. Until then, I carried on with life. Going to school was difficult. Why did this 10-page essay matter when I'd probably be dead in a few weeks? Still, I went to class and put in minimal effort. I focused most of my time with my friends and family. They could tell something was wrong. They asked me constantly if I was okay, but I brushed it off. I told them I was tired and had a lot on my mind. I wasn't lying. I was dealing with a life-or-death situation that would alter the course of my life and possibly the world. I'm also always tired.

I tried my best not to think about it. The more I thought

about it, the more real it became. *I'll deal with it in a few weeks,* I told myself. Well, I was right. I'll never forget that day. It was a Monday, and I was watching tv on the couch with my roommates. My Dad sent me a text that made my heart fall through the floor.

"You have an envelope from the government." The world seemed to stop spinning. The room went quiet as I understood what his text meant; I was screwed. *It's only been TWO weeks,* I thought as I raced over to my Dad's house. Time seemed to slow down as I got closer and closer. I begged God for it to be anything but my passport, and more time to prepare. *Just one more week. I haven't taken any military training classes. I haven't studied any war tactics. I haven't even shot a gun yet! Just one more week, God, please!*

I got to my Dad's house after what felt like hours of driving, then rushed inside to see that envelope waiting for me on the kitchen table. *Please, please, please.* I begged God while opening it up. I pulled my passport out, then looked down at it. A smile grew on my face, and I began to laugh. I told myself,

"Welp. Here's my death certificate." I got home to find Aaron and Jackson waiting patiently in the living room—just themselves and a wall in front of them. I flashed them my passport, and their eyes widened.

"What are you going to do?" Jackson asked me. I shrugged my shoulders.

"Well, I guess I'm ordering my ticket." I sat down and ordered a round-trip flight to Budapest. My departure date-April 2nd, just five days away. Once it came time to hit purchase, I paused. Before making a major decision in my life, I take a minute to think. I weighed everything out, and sat between my two choices. It boiled down to one question- **What type of man do you want to be?** I looked to Ren on my left, then Aaron and Jackson on my right. I flipped through my passport, and stopped on the last page. It read,

"The cause of freedom is not the cause of a race or a sect, a party or a class- it is the cause of humankind, the very birthright of humanity."-Anna Julia Cooper.

I knew my answer. I knew what type of man I wanted to be. I wanted to be someone who protected the innocent and faced his enemies no matter the odds. I realized that the man that I wanted to be was the person that I'd always been. I've always been this way, and I always will. There was no denying it. I had to walk through hell. I always knew my moral beliefs would get me killed, but didn't think it would be like this. *Oh well. I'd rather die being me.*

I clicked the button to confirm my purchase, then Aaron and Jackson immediately went to their rooms. It was just Ren and me now. I made my decision; I'd have to live with it. A few seconds later, my dad texted me, asking why a trip to Hungary had been booked. I'd forgotten that he got notifications about my purchases. He was confused because I told him I was getting my passport for a trip to London, which wasn't a lie. My flight had a layover in London.

I called him and told him I'd be over in a minute to explain everything. I drove back, walked inside, then sat down across from my dad. I looked in his worried eyes while telling him my plan. He knew just as well as me that I wouldn't back down, but for an hour, he begged me not to leave. Ren was standing right beside him, looking at me. It was easier to break my father's heart than to let her die.

"You don't gotta go. You can help here." He pleaded over and over. I shook my head then said,

"No, Dad. That's not how war works. You can send all the supplies you want, but if someone's not there to do something with it, then it's pointless. I'm going, and you're not changing my mind. You don't have to support my decision, but I want you to support me." We both walked outside; my dad stopped me and asked,

"Whatcha gonna do bout Memaw?" I replied,

"If you're gonna make big-boy decisions, you gotta live with the big-boy consequences," We drove to my Memaw's house and sat in the living room. I couldn't look her in the eyes while explaining that her youngest grandchild was going to war. She cried softly, but not as much as me.

"I just thought I had more time. I'm sorry, Memaw, but I gotta do it." She protested like my dad, but I wouldn't budge. I'd sold my soul, and it was time for my reward, "My flight leaves Saturday. If y'all want to see me off, you can. Dad, will you drive me?" My dad hesitated for a moment then responded,

"I can't. I have work." It broke me. My dad didn't want to see me before I went off and died. I muttered just one word,

"Okay." I understood why he didn't want to. He was trying everything possible to stop his son from dying. I love my Dad, he's the best dad in the world, but it still shattered my heart. We stood up, and the three of us hugged. As we hugged, my dad said a prayer. He asked God to help us through this hard time, and to watch over me. When he finished, he asked me again to reconsider, but it was pointless. I told him,

"Dad, it's set in stone. There's no going back." I turned to my memaw, then put my hands on her shoulders. I looked her in the eyes, tears flowing down my face, then said,

"I don't know how long I'm gonna be gone, Memaw, but I probably won't be back for your birthday. I went ahead and bought your present. I got it in my closet at home. When I get back, I'll give it to you. Okay Memaw? Can you just wait for me to come home?" She nodded, then I hugged her tightly. The thoughts of my friends and family laying dead in a field was what made me finally let her go. I left my memaw's house, knowing it would be the last time I saw them.

When I got home, I spent the rest of the day crying in my room. All the while, cursing myself and God. *Why are you doing this to me God? Why did you have to make me this way? Why did you have to make me love people so much? I'm going to die! I'm twenty years old. I have so much life to live. Why me?* I cried all night. It turned out to be the best decision I made that week. I cried until I couldn't cry anymore. Once it was over, I took a deep breath and looked in the mirror.

"Okay. It's over. It's done. You have to prepare. You have to stay strong and keep moving forward. That's the only chance you have of coming home. These next few months are going to be absolute hell and nothing less. I'm walking into hell, and doing it with a smile. Let's get it started." But not before one last attempt to get out of it. The next day is not a day I'm proud of. I decided to try something I'd never done before- overdose. I made a promise with myself that if I survived, I was going to war, and if not, well you know. I know you're judging me, but would you rather take the easy way out or go to war?

I took six grams of magic mushrooms, nine shots of whiskey, smoked four bowls of weed, drank three energy drinks, then downed some painkillers and adderall. All while puffing a cigar. Over seven substances in my body all at once, and I can't tell you a single memory of it. I woke up the next day staring at the ceiling, wondering why I was alive. But the deal was made, it was time to get serious.

That week was one of the worst weeks of my life. Every day was a rush to get ready, but I soon found out there was no preparation for war. I dropped out of school, which was an obstacle on its own. My school guidance counselor told me I couldn't drop out unless all my professors and their superiors gave permission. I reached out to my professors in hopes of getting them to sign my drop out forms, but all this did was waste more time. I told a few of my classroom friends what I was doing, as well as some of my teachers. They had mixed responses; two of my professors accepted it, the other one was furious so he asked me to speak privately in his office. He said he wouldn't sign my paper till I complied. I walked in and said,

"I don't have time for this. I'm leaving for war in three days, just sign the paper." He stood up in rage then yelled,

"I'm not signing anything till you sit down and we talk about this."

"Fine then!" I left his office to put it simply. Regardless, they respected my wishes and didn't tell the other students what I was doing. It took three days to ask everyone for their permission. When I finally got done, I went to turn in what I had, but the lady at the desk told me I didn't need to do any of that. She said the school does that to make the students reconsider, but I could've just dropped out online. To the person who made me do it, thank you for wasting three days I could have used to prepare for war. I went around that week talking to all my closest friends. It was all the same, 'You're stupid, you're going to die, I don't support you.' After making my grandma cry, none of it bothered me.

All but a few. We'll call her Post because that was my nickname for her. She was my coworker before I quit my job. How I felt about her was pretty clear, and I'm 100% sure she knew. She was just waiting for me to ask her out, either to say yes or no. I wasn't sure at the time. I never asked her out because I didn't want to hurt her. I knew I would eventually do something reckless and end up breaking her heart.

I called her one late night. I knew she was the only one who could make me stay. If she had asked me to stay, I would have, and I wanted her to. She didn't answer the first time, so I called again. She didn't answer. She texted me, explaining she was on vacation with her family. I asked her to call me back, but she said she was out with them, then told me to explain what was going on. I put it bluntly.

"Post, I'm going to Ukraine. My flight leaves Saturday." She replied,

"To do what?" I responded with,

"To fight." She began to type then stopped. I called and texted her repeatedly, begging her to talk to me, but she never responded. She ghosted me, and I felt the last bits of my heart break as I stared at 'delivered'. I didn't cry, but only because there were no tears left. I just wanted to tell her how I felt and see how she would react. Maybe she would have asked me to stay, maybe she would have said, 'I don't care.' Who knows. I stared at that word for hours. *Delivered. Delivered. Delivered.* I muttered it over and over in my head. *I just wanted to tell her how I felt and that I wasn't leaving her. She didn't even care enough about me to say goodbye. She just went ahead and wrote me off as dead like everyone else.* In a bit of rage, I tossed my phone onto my bed, then yelled,

"I'll show her! I'll show her how wrong she is! I'm going to survive and rub it in her face. I'll rub it in everyone's face!" My anger towards the war was righteous, but this anger was different. It was hateful anger. Anger against everyone who didn't support me. Anger against Putin. Anger against how cruel the world was. I felt it burning inside me. Until then, I suppressed it, but I let it out. I knew it was a mistake, but I didn't care. I would use whatever tools I could to push forward, no matter how much it would consume my heart.

The next one I spoke with was my brother Drew. He called me and told me to come over so we could work this Ukraine situation out. For hours, we sat on his back porch as he begged me not to go. All the while, drunk out of his mind. He said everything I've already heard before, but one thing different from everyone else.

"What are you going to do when you come across a Russian? What, kill him? You're not a killer, Peyton." I waited a minute to respond.

"I'm not sure if I'm a killer. I'm not goin' for that. The only person I wanna kill is Putin. I'm just goin' to help Ukraine, but if it means killing, then I'll do it. This is war. I get that. If it comes down to it, I know I'll do it. Just hope it doesn't." I said while staring coldly into his eyes.

"You don't have it in you to kill." He retorted. In a rage, I replied,

"You don't know what I'm capable of. None of you do. You'll all see." Drew kept on trying to convince me, but it was pointless. I'm as stubborn as a bull. Still, it hurt to see him in such disarray. I wanted to agree, but I looked over his shoulder to keep eye contact with Ren. Her clenching Ruby got me through the conversation. I knew I was making the right decision. Once it was over, I hugged him and his wife then left. I asked him to see me off at the airport, but it was the same with my dad.

After that, I stopped at my mom's house. We're pretty estranged and not on the best terms, however, a mother should see her son before he leaves for war. Telling our history would explain a lot why I am the way I am, but I won't do that. Our relationship is complicated, but I'm not going to put the woman who gave birth to me on full blast for the world to see. My mom is a good person at heart and deserves to be respected. She has made many mistakes, but I don't know of anyone alive who hasn't. Our conversation was quick because I was in a rush. I told her I was going, then she said,

"I had a feeling you would. I understand, baby. It's awful what they're doing. Do what you gotta do." I hugged her, got in my car, then drove back home. I wanted my dad to drive me, but without him, my next stop was my best friend and roommate, Jackson. I asked him to drive me, knowing he wasn't working that day, but he looked me dead in the eye and said,

"No. I'm not driving you."

"Jackson, you don't have to support my decision, but I want you to support me." Of anyone, I thought Jackson would, but I was wrong.

"That's the thing, I don't support you. I'm not supporting you getting yourself killed, and I'm not going to be a part of it." I thought for a moment before responding.

"Jackson, I'm doing it no matter what. I just want you to be there. You're my brother."

"Yeah, well, brothers don't abandon each other," Jackson went silent, then added, "You know, I didn't understand your speech that day. You know I haven't watched Naruto. You've tried to get me to for a year now, but I kept pushing it off. Now we'll never watch it." I gave a weak smile then said,

"Well, when I get back, we'll watch it." Jackson scoffed, stood up, then walked to his room while saying,

"No. It's not gonna happen." After all the pain that week, I was numb. I just said, 'Okay,' then continued with my preparations. Things were more tense in our apartment after that conversation. They distanced themselves from me once I bought that ticket, but I couldn't say anything; I did the same.

I needed to see my other mom before leaving, my sophomore English teacher, Mrs. Roshon. I'd grown up with her son Connor, and when we got to high school, she became my mom. There were a lot of problems going on at home, so I acted out in school because of it. I was the class clown; loved making people laugh to cover up my sadness. Being at school was the only place I could be happy, so I wanted to make it count. She had multiple reasons to send me to the principal's office, but never did. One day, while I was disrupting the class, she asked to talk to me outside. When we got outside, she said,

"Peyton, you're a good, smart young man. I believe you're going to do great things. You have so much potential. I love you as a son, and it hurts to see you waste it. Can you please do better just for me?" And with that, I decided to do better. I wouldn't have survived till graduation if it hadn't been for her. She's my mom, and she deserved to see me off. I tried to keep a brave face as I told her, but I couldn't. All the negative things everyone said were getting to me, and I was spiraling. I said,

"I'm about to go get myself killed, and there's nothing I can do. I don't have a choice. Mom, I'm gonna die." She put her hands on my cheeks, looked me dead in the eyes, then said,

"Peyton, if you don't listen to anything, listen to this. **If you think you're going to die, then you're going to die. The only way you're going to live is if you think positively.** Can you do that for me, sweetie?" I shook my head and hugged her. She was right. All those negative thoughts were just going to get me killed. Shortly after seeing my old football coaches and the principal, I left to meet my other brother, Mikey. He wanted to meet with me one last time. We met at Chuy's in Murfreesboro, and when we sat down, he said bluntly,

"I'm not here to talk you out of it. There's nothing I can say that will change your mind. You've already heard it. I just want to eat with my baby brother one last time." Mikey always understood me better than the rest of my family. We were both black sheep. Still, he had his own opinions,

"I think you're a traitor. Abandoning your country to help another one. One you have no ties to. I get it. I do. You've always wanted to help people, but you could help your people here. Ones who would do the same if you were in danger." Still, he was like me and understood it wasn't just about helping people. It was more than that. People are too complex for every decision to be completely selfish or selfless. He said the same thing that I was telling myself,

"I just want to see if you can make it." I wanted to see what I was capable of; how far I'd go. 'Can an inexperienced, autistic, twenty year-old college kid go to war all by himself?' Every kid tells themselves that when they get older, they're going to travel the world and do the impossible. But when you turn 18, it's college or work. All the fun and adventure you promised yourself doesn't come. The truth was, I was bored. Bored out of my mind. Nothing excited me anymore. Going to a party is fun the first two, maybe three times. But so what? You're just sitting around with a bunch of people you don't care about.

I found out the only thing that did bring excitement was life-or-death situations. Every time I'd hear shootings outside my apartment, I'd run outside, hoping to take down a gunman. Every time I saw smoke, I would run over and see if there was fire for me to run into. I wanted to help people, but it was also the only thing that interested me. It's why every cop is a cop. Sure, they want to help people, but they're just bored and want to do something interesting with a purpose. I went to Ukraine mainly to help, but at least 25% of it was because I was bored. I really did go to war because there wasn't anything interesting on TV, huh?

It wasn't just those reasons though. I was a lazy, powerless, poor, crybaby college kid who knew he was destined for more but didn't know how to obtain it. I knew war would change me, but change is what I needed, and this seemed like the best opportunity. I had to toughen up, and that was one thing war made sure to do. After we talked, I asked my brother to drive me to the airport. I expected him to say no, but to my surprise, he agreed.

"Of course, I'll drive you. You're my brother." It meant a lot to me. Even though he didn't support my decision, he supported me. After we ate, we went outside and sat in his car for hours, enjoying what time we had left. We smoked as we talked. For those who just judged me, I'll ask you to finish this book then see how you feel. He asked me if I wanted to test drive his car, but I told him I didn't know how to drive a stick. He replied,

"Well, WHEN you get back from the war, I'll teach you. Sound like a plan?" It might not have seemed like a lot, but what he said meant a lot to me. He believed in me. I smiled back and said,

"Sure. Sounds like a plan." After leaving Mikey, I went to the store and bought supplies. I anticipated I wouldn't have food during the war, so I stocked up on rations. I made thirty tiny bags, each with 500 calories worth of beef sticks and protein bars. In addition, I bought:

Med kit, backpack, solar-paneled rechargeable battery, pain pills, bandages, iPhone chargers, military boots, baby wipes, military pants, sleeping bag, watch, winter jacket, and a bag of rubber bands.

The rubber bands were for my self-control. Whenever I felt negative emotions, I slapped my wrist with the rubber band to snap myself back to reality. Is it unusual? Yes, but it did what it was supposed to do. Desperate times call for desperate measures. The baby wipes were a suggestion from my friend Damian. He fought in the Afghanistan war, so he seemed like the best person to ask for advice. He told me that baby wipes are a necessity in combat. We met in our college library where he tried to convince me to stay by telling his stories of his time in Afghanistan.

"You don't understand how much war sucks. Nobody does. It's not all brave, stoic men dying for honor. It's mostly boys crying to go home, but you can't. In my platoon one night, we were ambushed from above. Half of our men started to cry, me included, and our platoon leader told us, 'It's okay. Just point your gun at them and shoot. Just shoot.' I was so scared. All I could think during the fight was, 'You don't even know me. How can you hate me?' We managed to win the fight, but all I could think about after was, 'That guy had plans tomorrow. He planned to go out to eat with his family and see his kids. Now, he can't. All because our leaders said that the other side needed to die.' And then we pulled out of Afghanistan. All my comrades and Afghanies who died, died for nothing."

He finally gave up after realizing I wouldn't fold. He advised me on war, then gave me his old military bag, which I was scared to take. I planned to be as inconspicuous as possible, and an American with a military bag isn't. However, it was the only bag that could hold all my stuff. It was a difficult choice, but I decided on his bag.

After leaving Damian, there was nothing left for me to do on campus, so I walked around MTSU. It had been my home for the past two years, so I wanted to see it one last time. After finishing my walk, I stopped in front of the big blue horseshoe. Those who touch are granted good luck, or so the plaque says. I'd touch it before every semester, every test, every date. I put both hands on the horseshoe then thought, *I'm shootin' for the moon in a damn wheelbarrow. Lord knows I need all the luck in the world right now.* As soon as I let go, my life as a college student ended.

That night, I took a break to scroll through Facebook, and saw a post that rocked my world. It was a repost from over a year ago, and it was of a funeral service of my childhood friend Tyler. Tyler and I were in Boy Scouts when we were children. We'd grown up together all through school, and even though we grew apart after high school, I'd always considered him a brother. I was in disbelief, and what tears I thought were gone had come back. He'd committed suicide after years of battling with his mental health, and I did nothing. Tyler would have given you the shirt off his back, and I couldn't even give him a phone call once a month. It took me a year to even know that he'd died. I cried for hours until it was all out, then stood up and told myself,

He wouldn't want me to cry. He'd cheer me on and tell me to keep moving forward. I will, Tyler. I'll do it no matter what. Please watch over me, and if things go south, I'll see you soon. We'll fly kites and practice our knots like in the old days. I'll make this journey for you, too. Despite another heartbreak, I still had to continue my preparations.

I downloaded a language translator app that worked without WiFi. It wasn't the best, but something is better than nothing. I also downloaded all my songs so I'd have something to help keep me sane. My solar panel rechargeable battery meant that I'd have my phone as long as there was the sun. I figured that if I had access to my phone, I'd have an edge on my enemies. If I planned enough, then maybe I could come out on top, or at least not die.

My entire week was a rush to get ready. There were so many goodbyes, so many errands, and so much bullshit. But by Friday night, I managed to get everything done that was necessary. I didn't take any military or firearm training, but there wasn't enough time. I prioritized saying goodbye to my loved ones and getting my equipment. Besides, the best training is hands-on training anyway. It took me several hours to pack my bags. It was difficult to choose what was needed for war, and Ren's annoying suggestions didn't help either.

"No, Ren, we can't bring my ps4. What do you expect me to do with it? Throw it at the Russians?" Ren groaned from my bed as I struggled to stuff everything inside Damian's military bag. She leaped off my bed then handed me Ruby.

"Well, how about her?" She asked excitedly. I looked down at Ruby, then up at her big blue eyes. I couldn't say no.

"Sure, Ruby can come. She's small so she won't take up much space." I tucked Ruby into my food bag that would be my carry on. I didn't sleep much that night. I stayed up thinking about every situation that could happen during the war. By early morning, my wrist was blood red with all the slaps from my rubber band. Still, I knew that confidence was going to be my greatest strength.

"I am drastically under-prepared, but that doesn't matter. I'm clever, I'm resourceful, and I'm brave. If I'm not as strong as them, then I gotta be smarter than them." After several days of hell, it was finally Saturday. I was in a daze. It felt as if the world had stopped spinning just for me, just so I could finally sign away my life. My brother called me; it was time to go.

I went to my room and held each of my guinea pigs one last time. It was hard to let them go. They were my children, and leaving them was one of the toughest moments of that week. I had two- Xavier and Tony. Xavier is the son of Midnight and just as sweet. I'd raised him from the day he was born. Unlike Midnight, who I viewed as my brother, he was my child. I bought Tony from the pet store to keep Xavier company, but I loved him the same. I was leaving behind my children and my dreams. I dreamed of building a sanctuary for their children. I'd build it so that no predator could enter; where they could frolic in the fields without fear. As I kissed them both goodbye, I realized I was kissing away that dream and every dream I had. *War is where dreams go to die, so freedom can be born from the ashes,* I thought as I hugged each of them one last time,

"Alrighty. Daddy has to go kill some Russians. I'll be back real soon. Love you." I gave them one last kiss then put them back in their cage. I took one last look around my room. I'd recently read a book in my fantasy literature class called 'The Book of Three.' In the end, the main character, Taren, goes home and tells Dalvin that his room feels smaller. I wondered if the same thing would happen to me if I came back. I gave Aaron and Jackson one last hug and headed for the door.

"I'll see y'all when I see y'all." I gave a Luke Skywalker wave with my two fingers then left. Apartment A32 was no longer my home. I got in Mikey's car, and he handed me a cigarette. I lit it and smoked all the way to the airport. Mikey had just gotten off a 20-hour shift, and I knew he wasn't in the mood to talk. I wasn't either. I was playing every scenario over in my head. Every bad thought came with a slap on my wrist, bringing me back to reality. The drive to the airport couldn't have been quicker. I begged God to slow down time just this once, but he seemed to only speed it up.

We were at the Nashville airport in no time, and my last chance to quit was there. Mikey didn't bother me as I contemplated. He wanted me to make the decision. I looked through the airport door and saw Ren inside, staring at me. Her little hands were pressed against the glass. She was waiting for me. *I'm not as useless as everyone says. My enemies are people. They're not Gods. I just gotta be smarter and more confident.* I thought about Matt Damon in The Martian. In the end, he says, 'You solve one problem, and then you solve another. Until you get to go home.' *I've just gotta solve a lot of problems. The first problem to solve is how to get out of the car.* I opened the car door then quickly shut it behind me, along with all my hopes and dreams. My brother smiled then said,

"Don't die." All I could do was smirk.

"I promise," I replied. I took one deep breath then smiled as I walked into the airport. Ren walked up to me. Her cheeks were red like the rising sun. Tears began to flow down her cheeks, and at the time, I didn't know why. I kneeled on one knee and rubbed the tears from her eyes.

"It's okay. It's gonna be okay," she wrapped my hands with hers, "We're in this together to the very end. I won't turn my back on you—not now, not ever. I promise, and that's a Peyton promise. Those can't be broken. So Ren, will you be my travel buddy?"

"Okay." She softly replied while trying to hold back tears. She let go of my hand and swiftly wrapped her short arms around me. I hugged her, and we embraced for a moment before I let go. I took her by the hand, then we moved towards hell together.

4

NOTHING GOES WRONG

"Trip to Hungary, huh? Doesn't it border Ukraine?" The woman at the check-in counter asked with a smile. Right away, my plan to be a ghost would not work. The woman winked, making Ren giggle. I glared at her then mouthed, 'Shut UP!' before turning my attention back to the woman.

"Ukraine? Oh, I didn't know that. That's CRAZY. I'll make sure to stay away." I handed her my military bag, then she laid it on the conveyor belt. As it rolled away behind the curtains, my gut gave me a bad feeling they would lose it. But it was too late; it was gone. The Nashville airport is pretty small, not nearly as big as I expected. I thought we'd be in customs for hours, but we were out after twenty minutes. After getting through, we found our gate then waited to depart. We arrived three hours early, so we had plenty of time to kill. As we waited, I figured it wouldn't hurt to prepare.

I looked up YouTube videos of how to patch wounds, shoot guns, and maneuver through battlefields. Instead of just watching them, I downloaded them to my phone. I still wasn't trained, but I had the information available. Better than nothing, right? As I worked, Ren played around in the waiting area. I'd look up from my phone every few minutes to see her twirling around or petting someone's emotional support dog.

The clock hit three, our departure time, but nothing was declared. Just a few minutes later, we got word our flight was delayed. That bad feeling sank in again, I knew it would get canceled. After another three hours of waiting, the news came just as expected, so I banged my head on the brick wall behind me. Reality began to set in, *Of course it's canceled. There's no way it could be this easy.* My head turned towards Ren.

"This is gonna take a while, isn't it?" She looked up towards me with her big blue eyes, cocked her head to the side, then smiled. I groaned, then messaged my friends and family about what had happened. They all said the same thing, 'Maybe it's a sign for you not to go.' Despite all of this, there was still nothing going to stop me. In a rage, I replied,

"Maybe it's a sign of what's to come. Maybe this is my first test to see how committed I am. Who are you to determine what this sign means? You're just a coward too afraid to do the right thing. Of course, you'd read it that way." I didn't get a lot of positive replies after that, but I couldn't care less. It was my life on the line, not theirs. For hours, we waited for our flight. After so long, I got bored and began to walk around. Ren wanted to come, so I lifted her onto my shoulders and carried her around the airport. At each gift shop we passed, she tugged on my ears and cried,

"Here. HERE!" We'd walk in and analyze every object in the store. I've never been one for window shopping, but Ren was enthralled by everything she saw. She begged me to buy her a Nashville shirt at one shop, but I explained that thirty dollars for a t-shirt was criminal. She huffed, then stormed out of the store. I began to chase after her, but didn't make it two steps before feeling a tap on my lower back.

"Behind you." Ren cheerily remarked. I'd forgotten she could never leave me, no matter how much I sometimes wanted her to. At 8 o'clock, our flight was ready. It turns out our pilot and dozens of others from the airline company went on strike. They were protesting for better pay all across America, and of course it had to happen when I decided to leave. We had a new pilot and plane, but there was another problem. The communication panel on the plane was broken, and they didn't know how to fix it. For the next three hours we waited for news. I must have carried Ren 10 laps around that airport to keep my nerves at ease. I knew God would throw challenges in my way, but I wasn't expecting one right at the start. I tried to keep my spirits up the best I could.

"It's just more time for me to prepare," I told myself, as I followed along the floor patterns, making sure not to fall off their white lines. All the while, Ren swayed side to side to throw off my balance. I walked back to our gate, and found a group of people surrounding a teenage girl as she leaned against a pillar. Two older women were trying to comfort her, but she was inconsolable. I overheard her story from the people around- her father had a heart attack that morning, and needed to have surgery. However, he refused to die until he saw his daughter. The daughter found the quickest flight available, and was supposed to be at the hospital in New York at 6. At 9 o'clock the doctors said they couldn't wait any longer, and started the surgery. It was now 11 o'clock, the surgery was over, and her father didn't make it.

As I watched that girl sob, I could only think about all those pilots who went on strike for better pay, and their bosses who refused to give it to them. That girl didn't get to see her father, and her father lost precious time waiting for her. Just because you wanted a pay increase on your 6 figure job. It happened to them, and all across America. For those who were involved in the strike, all I have to ask is-was it worth it?

Our flight group was the only one in that airport, because apparently airports close. Once they announced we were boarding, everyone cheered. It was about damn time. We got on the plane, then Ren and I gave a sigh of relief. As we took off, our faces were glued to the window. As happy as I was to finally leave, I couldn't help but feel sad. I was leaving my home, and knew it would be a long time before seeing it again—if ever.

In no time, we were in New York. As we landed, I looked out my window in an attempt to see the Statue of Liberty, but it was 2 in the morning, and I had no idea where to even look. Once they gave us the okay to get off, we rushed out of the plane and I found myself completely out of my comfort zone. The JFK airport is enormous. It made the Nashville airport look like a convenience store in comparison. I was completely lost, so I followed a crucial rule when traveling- if you don't know where to go, follow the crowd.

We followed the crowd to the baggage pick-up center. It was chaotic. People were buzzing around everywhere, trying to figure out what to do. I looked to my right for Ren, but she was nowhere in sight. I checked every conveyor belt for my bag; as expected, it wasn't there. That wasn't my only problem. Since our flight was canceled, we missed the flight to London and needed a new ticket. It was 2 in the morning. I was alone in New York fending for myself with no bag, ticket, or sleep. I began to panic. Doubt started to sink in, and all those negative thoughts I'd been pushing out resurfaced. *What if everyone was right? What if this was a mistake? What if this is a sign to go home?*

I was being overstimulated, so I leaned against a wall as I started to hyperventilate. Right as I was about to pass out, I slapped the rubber band on my wrist. *Okay. Calm down. Even if I decided to go home, I'd need to fly out. And if I was to fly out, why not just keep going? I have to get a new ticket anyway, and they gotta give me one. I don't have my bag, but they gotta give me that too. It's just gonna take time. One problem at a time.* I got in the lost luggage line and waited until a woman announced,

"If you are missing your luggage, don't worry about it. Get your new ticket, and they will find your bag and send it to you." I got in line for a new ticket, then a tiny hand tugged on mine. It was Ren.

"Oh. You're back." Ren smirked, then we sat on the floor in the worst line I'd ever seen. We waited in that line for five hours. All the while trying not to fall asleep. We listened to the stories of the people around us. Several people had their vacations completely ruined and were trying to get back home. Some were crying because they were going to miss an important event. A few were like the girl; on the way to see someone before they passed, but didn't. It was the airport experience I expected, multiplied by 100.

After five hours of waiting, it was finally our turn. I was shaking in fear. Because of the sudden cancellations, several people couldn't get new flights. Some were told they'd have to wait several days for the next flight out. When they asked if the airport would pay for a hotel, they said,

"Here is a one-hundred dollar gift card for your next flight. For your troubles." I went up to the window, turned to Ren, then she gave me a thumbs up. I crossed my fingers, waited, and got lucky. There was an available flight leaving that night. I took my new ticket and sprinted away with Ren. We were finally free from our airport captor. The line had tripled since we entered and now wrapped around the room. I was thankful that our wait was only five hours.

We reached the entrance, then stepped outside to smell the New York air. It wasn't what I was expecting. It was raining; the smell gave off a rosy aroma, unlike the earthy smell in Tennessee. The air was also thinner than expected, not cleaner, but thinner.

After spending 15 minutes following a pigeon around, we went back inside. I was too scared to traverse New York on my own. Ironic, right? Too scared to walk around New York, but not a war zone. My good friend Oscar was from New York. He told me every New Yorker could spot a tourist from a mile away, and I had three grand in my pocket.

Besides, we were far too tired to do anything. We walked around the airport until we found the food court. We went up the stairs to the second story and found a table out of sight. Ren collapsed in the chair across from me. I set a timer, then laid my head down for a well-deserved nap. When my timer went off, I sprung up, unsure of where I was. I looked around and sighed while thinking, *Dammit, it wasn't a dream.* We still had time before the flight, so we went to the gift shop. I didn't have anything to remind me of America, and it seemed like a must when coming to New York.

"Okay, Ren. What do you want?" She put her index finger to her mouth and hummed as she examined everything in the store. She pointed at the shelf then yelled,

"This!" It was a Statue of Liberty keychain with 'Made in China' written on the back. *Just like home.* I thought. After paying for it, I tossed her the keychain, then said,

"This will be our lucky keychain. As long as we have it, we'll be safe," She jumped up and down as she cheered,

"Thank you, thank you, thank you!" I patted her on the head, pretending that I did it for her. I checked in with some difficulty. Instead of someone scanning my ticket, it was a do-it-yourself. After several tries and fails, I called customer support, and they got me situated. With nothing else to do, we explored the rest of the airport. While walking down a long hallway, I looked out the window and saw what I had always dreamed of,

"A TRAIN!" I shouted while pointing at the air train. At the JFK airport, they have a train that connects all the terminals. Ren looked at me in complete confusion.

"It's just a train." She replied matter of factly.

"Just a train? Just a train?! You're crazy, come on." I'd never been on a train before, so I looked like a kid in a candy store. I joyfully watched through the window as we took off. I didn't care how childish it seemed. I was going to be dead in a few weeks, and was going to enjoy every second possible. After eating at the food court, we went to our gate then waited until boarding. As the time drew closer, my doubt was rising. *The last flight went terribly; who's to say this one wouldn't?* But it wasn't just doubts about the flight. It was my first time leaving the country, my home. As a child, I dreamed of traveling the world, but we couldn't afford to. Now, it has cost me my life.

We boarded the plane, and were blown away by how high class it was. Every person had their bed, blanket, and a free meal to be delivered halfway through our flight. Ren disappeared again, but it didn't bother me. I was on the brink of collapse and was fighting to stay awake to do one last thing. I stripped off my extra clothes then watched as our plane slowly went down the runway. Once we were off the ground, I leaned back in my bed, shut my eyes, and whispered,

"Goodbye America." Within seconds, I was fast asleep and on my way to Europe. I awoke mid-flight to find a hostess with my food. After scarfing it down like a starving dog, I went back to sleep and didn't wake up until we arrived in London. My time in London was sadly uneventful. I'd always dreamed of visiting Britain, but knew my 2-hour layover wouldn't suffice. It was a rush getting to my flight. Still, it felt weird being in Europe. The atmosphere felt different, as did the English around me. Everyone spoke with a British accent, making me feel like I'd fallen into a Harry Potter book. I've always been an outsider, but now it felt even worse.

After making it through customs, our first stop was getting some fresh air. I was way too curious to know what Britain smelled like. We stepped outside, then inhaled its cold London fragrance. It was unlike anything I'd ever experienced. It smelled exactly how I expected it to smell, but it's hard to put into words. It smelled like a giant gray school building, if that makes any sense.

Getting through screening was stressful to say the least. With only 2 hours, it was a race against the clock, and the two-hundred people ahead did not give us much confidence. The line moved fast, though, and within thirty minutes, we could see the metal detector. However, their screening process was different. TSA asked to place all liquids and hygiene products in a clear plastic bag. Since I didn't have any, they just shook my bag and let me on through the metal detector. I reminded myself that in this country, 9/11 didn't happen, so flying was different.

We made it through screening then found our gate. We had thirty minutes to spare, so a large weight was let off my shoulders. Now that I discovered it existed, I told Ren to wait, while I went to the restroom. I did have some trouble. No, not that kind of trouble. After finishing my business, I reached for the knob to flush, but found nothing. For five minutes, I searched that stall before finally finding it on the back wall. I laughed while watching the water go down, then said,

"I struggle to flush a damn toilet. How the hell am I gonna

fend off the entire Russian army?" With my confidence shaken, I returned to the gate, then we boarded our plane. The plane looked 40 years old from the inside, which didn't bode much confidence. It was also very cramped, so Ren disappeared again. Still, I had a window seat and watched in awe as we flew over the English Channel, Poland, then Hungary. As we approached the ground, I could see Hungary for the first time. It looked like home, but different.

Once the plane landed, we went through customs then made our way to the bag pick up section. As expected, my bag was nowhere to be seen. While waiting in line at the help desk, I struck up a conversation with a British couple in front of us. The same had happened to them.

"Our pilot didn't show up, and now our vacation is ruined. We were supposed to go backpacking across Hungary this week." The woman proclaimed.

"Yeah," I said, "I had some serious plans this week too. Looks like it's gonna be a while." The man was in his late thirties and looked at me confused.

"Excuse me, you said you're twenty, right? What are you doing all on your own here?" Ren nudged my hand, but I didn't look down. It was time for my cover story that I'd been practicing.

"I'm here to visit my girlfriend. Her father is American, and her mother is Hungarian. She moved here last year, and I told her I'd visit. We're trying to make it work." The man gave me a curious look, but the help desk opened up, and he went ahead. After he was done, I stepped up to fill out a form about my lost bag. After handing it back, the woman behind the desk said,

"It be. Two to four days. Before you get bag. We call when it arrive." *You've got to be kidding me.* I thanked the woman then slumped onwards. I couldn't leave without my military bag, so we were stuck in Budapest until it arrived. *Where the hell are we actually?* I checked my map, and found we weren't actually in Budapest, but a city nearby named Vecsés. I lifted Ren onto my shoulders and said,

"I guess we better start walking then. We've got some time to kill." I handed Ren my food bag then walked through the sliding glass doors into Hungary. I was finally in Europe, the Old World; free to explore it with Ren.

5

CALM BEFORE THE STORM

I looked on Google Maps to check our surroundings. I needed to find a hotel, but there was one major problem —my phone had 10% battery and I didn't have a European charger. My first objective was to get one. We followed a walking trail that connected the airport to Vecsés. While we walked, I took in our surroundings.

"We're really in Europe, huh, Ren? It doesn't feel real." Ren skipped along the path, humming an upbeat tune while I examined every ounce of life. Everything looked the same but different, as if I'd landed in a parallel world. The craziest thing is, Hungary smelled almost exactly like home. It made sense why Grandpa Freed settled in Tennessee. I felt at home in Hungary despite how drastically different it was.

"Look, Ren!" I pointed towards a large McDonald's sign hanging in the sky, "American safe space!" The McDonald's was the first building entering the city, and I couldn't have been happier. After crossing a roundabout, we walked towards the McDonald's. Sadly, this wasn't our first stop. On my map, it showed a shopping mall nearby, and I knew we could get our supplies there.

We found our way to a store called Praktiker. When we walked in, I saw the giant beams of wood and gardening tools for sale, so I knew it was the right spot. This was their version of Lowes. I found an employee and used my translator app to ask for help. I found the charger then checked out at the desk.

We went into a store called H&H a few stores down then purchased some clothes. One of the reasons I chose Hungary, besides its border, was its lower GDP. Two T-shirts, two sweatpants, and a pair of socks only cost me 10 dollars. I was blown away at the notification. I knew the American dollar was worth more in other countries, but I wasn't expecting that.

Next, we went to Tesco, which is their version of Walmart, to buy hygiene products. Finding the shampoo took me a while because they don't use the word shampoo. They use the word milk instead. In my arrogance, I bought the cheapest shampoo possible. A horrible decision I'd regret for weeks. I also needed to wash my clothes while on the move, so I improvised. I got a bottle of Dawn dish soap and hoped for the best. After getting everything I needed, we went to McDonald's.

As expected, the food was cheap. I was able to get a Big Mac meal, and a 10 piece nugget for Ren, for under 10 dollars. I hadn't seen those prices since I was a kid. Once we got our food, I charged my phone, then called my credit card company. I wanted to clarify that it was me making the purchases. They assured me they would know if it was fraud, but being half-way across the globe didn't flag anything; a terrifying thought.

After my phone had enough charge, I picked up Ren then headed towards the nearest hotel, the Budapest Airport Hotel. Ironic, considering that it wasn't actually in Budapest. I was blown away by how elegant it was when we walked inside. It was as if we'd walked into a mansion. After checking in, we went to our room. After changing, I took my dirty clothes into the bathroom, washed them with Dawn dish soap in the shower, then set them on an electric drying rack. For those who don't know what those are, I don't blame you. They're plastic rods on which you place clothes, and when you start the machine, it heats them. I'd never seen one before, but it is a very nice tool. After getting done, I went into the bedroom to find Ren jumping on the bed.

"Ren, no one can hear you, but you still gotta be courteous." She pouted then did one last jump before crashing onto the pillows.

"What ya gonna do now?" She asked as she tossed a pillow at me. I knocked it away and glared at her.

"It's time to tell my people how stupid I am." I set my phone on the desk and began recording videos then posting them onto a private story on Snapchat. My viewers consisted of my family, and everyone I'd been friends with through the years, amounting to over 100 people. I explained everything to them, all the way up to checking into the hotel. I was pretty transparent because lying didn't matter anymore.

"I'm doing these videos for y'all because this is the end of my story, and y'all deserve to know how it ends. At least as much as I can show. So many of y'all have given me so much; the least I can do is give you one last story. I know how bored y'all are." I knew it was cruel. I made 100 people wake up daily wondering if I was alive, but it was more about me than them. I was so alone and scared that the thought of my closest friends and family watching and cheering me on made me not feel so alone, "Well, I'm gonna be dead in a few weeks, so I'm gonna enjoy them. I'm gonna go get my first legal drink. Imma catch y'all later." I turned to Ren, who was lost in space.

"Are you done yet?" She asked with a yawn.

"Yeah, but Imma go drink. I'll be back in an hour or two. Here's the tv remote." She frowned while nodding her head. I went to the bar then ordered my first legal drink- Vodka. I mixed it with OJ, then drank while trying to avoid conversation with the bartender. He looked like the scientist from Iron Man and acted just as sincere. He didn't probe me for information, even though he was obviously curious. I drank until the room started to move sideways. It was then I realized all my fear, all my hate, and all my sadness was gone. I was happy. For the first time in weeks, I was actually happy.

I thanked the bartender then stumbled up the stairs to my room. Once inside, I collapsed onto the bed. Ren was fast asleep with Ruby in the guest room, so I slept in the main. It was my first time sleeping in a bed in a few days; it felt like it was my first time ever. As I slowly drifted to sleep, I thought, *I'd be the happiest man on Earth if I never woke up.*

I awoke the next morning to Ren inches from my face. I moved back, banged my head against the wall, then yelled at her as she giggled. I went to the bathroom to check on my clothes. They smelled good, weren't wrinkled, and were dry. *Soap is soap,* I chanted inside my mind. After showering then getting dressed, we ate their complimentary breakfast downstairs. It was a typical breakfast buffet, although it felt more high class. I nodded to the front desk woman then headed out. I had one priority- get a knife.

Using Google Maps, I navigated us across the city to a knife store. Along the way, I learned that different countries prefer different colors. It was apparent that Hungary preferred brown and yellow. I bought a tiny knife, only slightly bigger than my hand. I didn't know what to name my trusty companion, so I turned to Ren.

"Alrighty Ren, since you did a good job naming Ruby, what should I name our knife?" She put her hands to her temple as she thought. As she did, a man on a motorcycle passed by, and her eyes lit up.

"Rider." She proclaimed as she pointed to the knife.

"Rider it is," I looked down at Rider while thinking about my future, "This knife will save the world. I just know it." It would, but not in the way I thought. While in town, I stopped at a gas station and picked up a few cartons of cigarettes, much to Ren's dislike. She put her hands on her hips then scowled at me, but I brushed it off.

"Once you lose all of your friends and family and go to war with nothing but a knife, then you can judge me. Until then." I lit my cigarette then started down the street. I was too scared to walk around the city alone, so we returned to the airport to ask about my bag. After getting an obvious no, we walked down the bike trail then into a forest nearby. We found an old tree in an open field for us to rest under. I stared at the sky while thinking about the war and my plans as Ren dozed off. *What's plan C? What's plan D?* I closed my eyes then began to brainstorm. In my head, I went over every possible situation, every battle strategy; anything that could give me an edge. *A man who plans is a man who succeeds. Plan C is simple, not much different from plan B, but I can't help much with it. If they both fail, what am I gonna do? What's my strengths? What can an American in a foreign country do-*

Then it hit me. I shot up as if an explosion had been set off. The wind seemed to have gotten colder and the sky darker. I began to hyperventilate as the images of my plan swept across my mind. It was so clear. I curled into a ball as the pictures flashed faster and faster. Tears that I didn't know I had left came out. The feeling inside me that I would decide humanity's fate, was true. Destiny pulled me to choose, and Plan D would do it. I held the fate of humanity in the palms of my hands, and it was heavy.

"I'm sorry. I'm so sorry." I clenched the grass and cried until Ren nudged me on the shoulder.

"Are you okay?" She asked. I looked up at her worried eyes then slapped my wrist with my rubber band. I crawled on my knees closer to her then bowed my head.

"Yeah, I'll be fine. Let's go." I put her on my shoulders, then we started walking back to the hotel. I thought about the future the entire time and prayed that it was wrong. If plan B went up in flames, I'd have to make plan C work. If not, I'd resort to plan D- the end of humanity.

That night, I made a beer run. I didn't want to pay for the hotel bar, and also wanted to drink alone in my room. I told Ren I was leaving for some air then ordered a taxi. It turns out that Uber doesn't work in Europe, and after some Google searches, found that Europe uses an app called Bolt. It was my first time ordering a taxi, but it's so simple a child could figure it out. Once I sat inside the man's car, he began to speak to me in Hungarian, but I shook my head.

"I American." I declared. He nodded, then we drove on. As we drove, he kept giving me curious looks as if there was a monkey on my head. Finally, he asked,

"What you do here? You look young to travel alone." He caught me off guard, so I pretended to not understand him. This is a valuable tactic when dealing with a language barrier. He repeated himself, and I replied,

"My girlfriend. She lives in Lónya. I come to see her." I could have simply said Budapest, but no. I had to say Lónya. The driver gave a crooked smile.

"Ahh. Lónya. I UNDERSTAND." I clenched Rider for dear life, however, there was no need. The driver became friendlier and drove me to a closer liquor store. He asked if I needed help, but I shoved it off. I had to get used to speaking with foreigners. I went inside their small liquor store to buy a case of beer using my translator and hand signs.

When I came out, the driver ran across the street and walked me across like my bodyguard. As we drove back, we talked about America. He was very curious about football and how it was played. An explanation I gave several times on my journey. When we got back, I got out of the car, then he said,

"Hey Peyton," his face turned serious. "You be careful. Seeing GIRLFRIEND. Yes?" I gave a weak smile with a thumbs up. He returned my gesture then drove away. That night, I stayed up late drinking and smoking as I gazed out into the Hungarian sky. All the while, I thought about my future, while Ren played a racing game on my phone.

"Peyty, I need help," Ren declared as she steered my phone from left to right, "I can't get past this level." I kept staring forward at the night sky, planning every scenario around Plan D.

"I can't. I'm busy." I took a puff from my cigarette, blew it upwards, and it covered the stars.

"Why are you so serious?" She asked me, not taking her eyes off the phone.

"In a few short weeks, I'm going to decide the fate of humanity. Billions of people could die depending on what I do. It's nothing to think lightly about." Ren went silent and put the phone down. She walked towards me then leaned against the rail. She looked up at the starry sky then at me.

"Well, if I knew what would happen in the future, I wouldn't be a mister grumpy pants. There's nothing I can change. The only thing I can change is how I feel until then." I patted her on the head then shoved my cigarette bud into an empty bottle.

"Yeah. You're right." She returned to her game, and I pulled up a chair beside her. We played for the rest of the night, so my mind didn't drift towards the future. For the first time in a long time, I was truly happy. The next day, I checked out of the hotel then we spent the rest of the day hiding in the woods or the shopping row. It was hard to ease our boredom because there wasn't much to do. Ren wanted to see the city, but walking around enemy territory would be a death wish. However, that night the solitude was starting to get to me, so I said, 'Screw it,' then we walked around the city hoping to find an open bar.

It was so quiet that it made my hometown feel like Nashville. I figured at least one bar would be open, but everything was closed. The empty streets also made me worry; my puny knife and invisible friend weren't enough to protect me. Defeated, I searched Google Maps for a hotel near the airport.

We walked back to the side of town with the airport, crossed some train tracks, then entered a dark gravel street. My map told us the hotel was right up the street, but no sign was visible. Not wanting to draw attention, I avoided using the flashlight on my phone, and we ventured into the darkness. We kept going until my map said we were a few feet away. To our left was a Pizza Plaza, and to our right was a car dealership. The Pizza Plaza felt like the best guess. We walked towards it then found a side road hidden beside it. We walked down the muddy road and saw the sign of the hotel.

We walked inside, and I felt a chill go down my spine. It was a small lobby with more plants than walking space. A TV was playing, but the volume was on mute. I went to get a better look then saw Two and a Half Men playing—only it had a Hungarian voiceover. A tall man in a black suit appeared behind the counter. After finding out I didn't speak English, he nodded and used hand signs for the rest of our conversation. He wrote my name down in a log book then handed me our key to the room. It was an old-fashioned metal key, unlike the key card from the previous hotel.

"A30. Down hall. Left." He said. I thanked him then we started down the long, quiet hallway. We were halfway to my room when we came to an opening. On both sides were windows with rocking chairs, and in the chairs were tiny porcelain dolls. I grabbed Ren by the arm and ran down the hall to our room.

"What's wrong?" She asked, but I was too busy figuring out the lock. I'd never used an old-school key before, and right when I needed to was the worst moment. I heard the click then we ran inside the room. After tossing Ren on the bed, I slammed the door behind us.

"Well, Ren, get comfortable because we're not leaving this room till mornin." I locked the door and placed my bag in its creeks. I pulled out Rider and checked every inch of the room. Once it was safe, I blew a sigh of relief and relaxed on the bed. The frame was made of fine oak and looked as if it was decades old. I looked at the TV stand and didn't see a flat screen but a box TV. I hadn't seen one since I was a kid, which made me feel young for a minute. Despite being further in the past, I preferred that hotel over the other, besides the creepy dolls.

The next morning, we ate their complimentary breakfast. After checking out, we walked on, happy not to have been murdered. We hung out in the woods, waiting for the phone call for the rest of the day. Finally, my phone rang in the afternoon. The lady told me my bag arrived, so we jolted to our feet.

"Finally!" I grabbed my food bag then we sprinted down the bike route towards the airport, "Ren, it's finally time! The days of waiting are over! It's time for war!" We ran to the airport and went inside. I needed to call her back, but my phone wouldn't work for some reason. After a difficult attempt at using a cord phone, I asked a nearby man for help by showing him the number I wanted to dial.

"I help you. One second." He answered his phone then stepped a few feet away. Once done, he slipped the phone into his coat pocket then stared off, pretending I didn't exist. I called him several insults in my head, then went to a cleaning lady for help. Her response,

"Well, why can't you do it yourself?" I'd never gotten a response so rude before, so I told her never mind, then walked away with my tail between my legs. I looked around, saw the Japanese help desk, and figured they had to speak English. I was right, and the man at the desk helped me dial the number. It turned out the number I had didn't include the area code, so my call wasn't going through. I learned a helpful tip- know which area code you're in.

I called the woman, then she came to meet me. We walked into the bag-holding area, and I saw it. On a metal cart was my military bag. I rushed over to it. As soon as I touched it, I felt a chunk of my freedom disappear. The woman stared at me in awe.

"Is this... your bag?" She asked, her body stiff as a board.

"Yes! Thank you!" I exclaimed with so much joy it felt like I was going to explode. I opened it up to look inside. Everything was accounted for, and it didn't look to have been tampered with. She waved me along, so we went towards security. As a female security guard approached, I set my bag on a table and stepped away. She looked at my bag, then at me. Her eyes said it all, 'Are you crazy?' I gave her the best American smile possible, then she called over some other security guards.

I stepped towards the nearest exit just in case things went south. They didn't touch my bag though. They talked among themselves for a few minutes while we waited. Eventually, they turned towards me then crossed their arms. The help desk woman walked up and cleared her throat.

"The security guards tell me, 'We refuse to search his bag.'

You can take your bag. I wish you luck." One of the security guards went towards the exit to hold it open. I was at a loss for words. I grabbed my bag then looked at the guards. I put my hand to my heart, bowed, then smirked. We went through the door, and as we left, the security guard gave me a thumbs up. I returned it, then we sprinted away, finally free to continue on our journey.

6

CITY OF SPAS

"**This is wonderful, Ren!**" I screamed as we ran down the bike route. "I feel like I'm on cloud 9 right now! Let's get some Mickey D's. Then we'll head out." Ren followed behind. Despite her short legs, she managed to keep up with me.

"McDonald's sounds good," she wheezed, "But can we walk there? My feet hurt." I slowed to a jog, turned, then picked her up in one swoop before continuing to a full sprint.

"We don't have time for walkin! We've got a train to catch." To no one's surprise, carrying a full military bag and a 40-pound girl didn't let me run for long. We weren't a quarter of the way before my legs gave out, so I crashed underneath a tree. Despite my gasps for air, I lit a cigarette then smiled while gazing off into the sky.

"Ren. It's finally time. We're gonna make it to Ukraine. These days in Vescés are over! By this time tomorrow, we'll be in Ukraine, and I'll be one step closer to saving you." Ren looked up then smiled, "Whatcha smilin' bout?" She refused to answer, and when I asked again, she erupted with laughter.

"You look so funny when you're happy." She managed to muster while giggling.

"Thanks. I'll take it as a compliment. Come on, let's keep moving." She pulled herself together and stood up, then we continued down the bike route. As we were walking up the stairs to the McDonald's, a middle-aged man was walking down, then stopped in front of us.

"Katona vagy?" He said while pointing at me. I turned to Ren, but she shrugged her shoulders.

"I American." I replied. His eyes lit up, and he pulled out his wallet.

"You go. Ukraine. Yes?" My body stiffened. My suspicions were right- I had a target on my back. I figured there was no point in hiding it. An American in Hungary toting a military bag is more obvious than OJ Simpson.

"Yes." I replied. The man pulled a wad of cash from his wallet, "No, no. I'm good."

"No! Take it." We went back and forth until the man finally understood how prideful and stubborn I was. I thanked him, then he shook my hand. He wished me good luck on my journey and told me to, 'Give. Them. Hell.' I nodded, then we walked inside. The McDonald's was filled with people. It might have been because of my past two encounters, but all eyes seemed to be on me. I ordered our food then found an empty table as secluded as possible.

While we waited for our food, I reminisced about the past few days. Our days in Vecsés are some of my favorite memories. It was my first time in Europe, as well as my first time truly free. No job, friends, family, college, or responsibilities. Just Ren and me. I was the freest man in the world. That liberty disappeared the moment I touched my bag. My responsibilities returned, as well as the time clock for my death.

After eating, we went outside and I smoked a cigarette. I waited until five before ordering us a taxi. My plan was simple: We'd take the train as far north as possible then walk to Lónya. There, I would change into my all-black gear then we'd cross the border at midnight. *Simple,* I told myself. However, nothing went as planned. When the taxi arrived, the driver glanced at my military bag then grinned.

"Good job! I military, too! Go. Get them!" He gave me a thumbs-up, then we flopped into the back seat. We drove into Budapest, and we saw the city for the first time. Since it was later at night, everything was dark. It was a lot less colorful than I expected. The typical yellow and brown was everywhere, but now it was mixed with gray. The street lamps were yellow, shocker, which made the dark colors even more grim. Still, it was breathtaking. Almost every building was made from stone and had a Gothic design. It was hard to grasp that many of these buildings were hundreds of years old, a common theme in the Old World.

The driver dropped us off at the train station, and we followed the crowd to the ticket-buying machines. Thankfully, there was an English option. Despite using my language, I had no idea what I was doing. After several tries and giggles from Ren, I learned how to purchase my ticket. It asked where I wanted to go, and when I googled Lónya, it wasn't available. The furthest north the train would take us was a city called Nyíregyháza. From my math, it was a 6-hour walk from there to Lónya. Very doable. I purchased my ticket and was unsure if I did it right, so I bought another just to be sure. It said my ticket would expire in 24 hours, and our train would leave at ten o'clock. I looked at my watch.

"Perfect. We've got a few hours to kill." I took Ren by the

hand, and we wandered onto the train platforms. It was marvelous. The ceiling was high with columns every few feet. Along the sides of the walls were beautiful murals that looked ancient. It was pretty bright unlike the darkness of the city. While walking down the platforms, I spotted a group of police officers standing outside one of the trains. My eyes widened, and I grabbed Ren's arm then sprinted away.

"What's wrong?" She asked, but we didn't have time. We ran out of the train station then onto the busy sidewalk, "Why did we run?"

"We can't trust the police. Not here," I said as I slumped along the brick wall then pulled a cigarette out, "Any one of them could be working for Russia. As soon as they see my military bag, I'm a goner. It's just best to stay in ghost mode for now." Ren pouted then plopped onto the ground. She rubbed her shoulders as she shivered. She gave me a stink eye, so I threw my hands up in the air.

"What do you want me to do?! I'm the one who dies or goes to jail. You just get to come and go as you please." She continued to pout as I smoked, making me finally cave, "Fine. We'll go find somewhere warm to hide." We walked around the train station until I saw a McDonald's sign. I knew that we'd be safe there.

We stepped inside, then my jaw dropped. It was as if we walked into a king's dining hall. A large chandelier hung from the ceiling, with marble columns in each corner. It was dimly lit, but enough to see around the room. Every employee wore a yellow ascot with a little black M along its center. The male workers wore suits, while the females wore skirts. It was the most high-class McDonald's I'd ever seen.

I found a lonesome table and we napped until it was time to leave. At 9:30, we took off towards the train station, but it wasn't as busy as before. We walked to the platform to find every train track empty. I looked down at Ren, who just shrugged her shoulders. We went outside and sat down on a bench. I spotted a train employee washing the steps with a garden hose. He moved closer to me then began to speak, but I shook my head.

"I American." He grunted then gave a frustrated sigh.

"Train station. Closed."

"But I have ticket." I replied while flashing it at him.

"Train Station. Closed. Leave!" I grabbed my bags then walked down the street with Ren. The city was empty. It was still lit, so we could see, but it was as if all life had escaped the city. I figured every major city was like New York, 'The city that never sleeps.' Especially Budapest, a place thousands of years old. But I was wrong. That was one of many lessons I learned that night.

"Ren, I don't understand." I plopped down on a bench then gazed into the black sky, "How could they print me a ticket for a train that wasn't coming? Stupid machine. And train stations close? That's new information." I would realize later, while drunk at night, my mistake. My stupid American brain forgot the rest of the world runs on military time. Not AM or PM. Since I bought the ticket late, it automatically printed me one for 10:00 the next day. You should've seen my face when I realized. I banged my head against a brick wall, calling myself an idiot for several minutes.

"What we gonna do?" Ren asked. I looked at the time. It was almost 10 p.m., sorry, 22 hundred. I was homeless, cold, and alone in enemy territory thousands of miles away from home. I pulled out a cigarette then lit it. I looked up towards the night sky while weighing our options. I could call a taxi and return to Vecsés, but I didn't want to waste money. We could walk back and camp in the woods, but it would be a 2-hour walk. At that point, we should just stay awake. My third and most obvious choice was to find somewhere to sleep in the city.

"God wouldn't let us leave Budapest without checking it out. No matter how much I didn't wanna risk it. He's got a funny sense of humor. Now I'm in even more danger than before." I couldn't help but laugh. **You either laugh or cry, and crying hasn't saved me yet.** I picked up my bags then we walked towards the nearest hotel.

I quickly learned another lesson that night- hotels close, and hotels get full. For an hour, we went to every hotel we could find. It was either locked or the employees said there were no rooms available. After the 5th hotel, I gave up then tried to sleep on a bench until morning. However, whenever someone walked past us, I'd spring back to life with Rider ready. It was also the end of winter, so the cool Budapest air made it too cold to sleep.

I finally caved and ordered a taxi to drive us to the cheapest hotel on the other side of town. As we neared the hotel, I felt I'd made a mistake. We exited the heart of the city then started down tight, dark alleyways. I have to give it to the driver. I rolled down my window then touched the building walls without fully extending my arms; he wasn't driving slow either. It was some of the best driving I'd ever seen.

We came to a torn-down stop sign on a walking strip. Several police officers and firefighters were investigating the scene several feet away. Dozens of people dressed in black leather walked in groups like schools of fish. I found out where all the people in the city were. I figured we were safe because police were nearby, but remembered how wrong I was. The driver told me we arrived, so we stepped out of the car.

We walked down the walking strip towards the hotel but were quickly disappointed. I saw a large, crowded dance floor with colorful blinking tiles. The hotel was a party hotel. I'd be lying if I said it wasn't a debate. It would've been my first clubbing experience; could've been a lot of fun, but I wasn't looking for fun. I was looking for a safe place for us to sleep before our dive into a war zone. We turned around, walked back outside, then leaned against the brick wall. I was debating our next move when a short man in a gray jacket approached me.

"Marijuana?" He asked. I turned to the cop a few yards away then back to him. I shook my head, then he walked on to the next person. A minute later, he returned and asked, "Coke?" I looked back at the police investigating the downed stop sign then back to him. He was either incredibly stupid or an undercover cop. Either way, I wasn't buying anything off him. He moved on, and I continued to look at hotels nearby.

We were ready to head out, when a woman came out of the club, then leaned against a wall while sobbing. She had long black hair, fair skin, and was dressed in full leather. She was alone and wasted. Unfit to walk, let alone defend herself. I don't leave women like that alone without offering help. I never have, and vowed I never would. There's nothing wrong in offering help if your intentions are pure. However, I was on a mission. *She's just gonna have to take care of herself.* I took a few steps then stopped. Ren was in front of me, staring me down with her hands on her hips.

"Ren, we don't have time for this. There's police right there. Nobody would try to hurt her." Ren pointed to the drug dealer walking from person to person then cocked her head with a smile, "She's a grown-ass woman. She can protect herself." I retorted. Ren pointed behind me. I turned and saw as she struggled to hold herself upright. She continued to sob louder and louder; I knew what the right thing to do was. I groaned then walked towards her.

"Hello. Are you okay? Do you understand me?" I asked while bending down on one knee to be eye level with her. The woman looked up at me then smiled.

"Yes. I speak English, and no. I am not okay." She spoke in broken English, but given she was incredibly drunk, it must've been incredible when sober.

"What's your name?"

"My name is Lala. And yours?" She asked.

"My name's Peyton. Why are you not okay if you don't mind me asking?" She wiped her tears then managed to stand up with the help of the wall.

"I just miss my boyfriend so much! He is not my boyfriend anymore. We dated in college, but he broke up with me! He said we could still be friends, and I said that was okay. I went out tonight to have fun. Inside I was dancing with another man. But it was not the same. I miss him so much. I love him. I don't want to feel this way. It hurts so much. Why does it have to hurt so much? Have you ever been in love? Do you understand how I feel?" Immediately, it made me think of Post. I set my bags down then leaned against the wall next to her.

"Yeah. I get what you mean. Love is painful. Sometimes, it makes you do stupid things. I know that way too well, but it's worth it. It makes us feel alive. Despite how much it hurts." I looked at my military bag, and thought about my friends and family as well as the innocents of Ukraine.

"I texted my boyfriend. He is coming to get me. He will be here in thirty minutes."

"If you don't mind, I'll stay here until he gets here," I replied, "If that's okay with you." She nodded, then we kept talking. For the next ten minutes, she went on and on about how much she loved her ex-boyfriend. She also told me about how she was from Syria and came to Budapest on a visa. She met her ex in a foreign-student class, and they were together until a few days ago. I tried to change the subject, so I asked about her major. She told me she studied communications, then asked what mine was.

"I was first a psychology major. Then, I changed it to political science. I dream of being president one day. But things happened, so I'm here now." She knit her eyebrows. Despite being drunk, my military bag still raised some concerns.

"Why are you here? You are so young to be traveling alone." I told myself to be a ghost, but at that moment, I didn't want to. I wanted to tell someone the truth for once. I've always hated lying; it killed me every time I did. I figured since she was drunk, she wouldn't remember what was said anyway.

"I'm going to Ukraine to fight in the war. I got my military bag from a friend. I don't plan on coming back to my country for a long time—if ever." I pulled out my cigarette carton then plucked a cigarette out. I offered her one, but she refused. Her face was filled with even more sorrow than before.

"You are so young. Too young to die. Too good to die." I laughed; her reply was ironic.

"Nobody is too young or too good to die. **The bones of good young people are the foundation of freedom.** It's just my turn to cast mine in. Love will make you do some CRAZY things." I let out a laugh as well as some smoke. Eventually, her ex showed up in a taxi. He gave me a handshake, nodded, and thanked me for watching over her. With a wave goodbye, they hopped in the car then took off. I'm not sure what happened to Lala, but I hope she's happy wherever she is.

Ren and I continued to look for hotels but got the same responses. It was midnight, and I was ready to admit defeat. I decided we'd spend the night in a bar. As we were walking, we found a bar then settled down at a table. It was empty, aside from two men at the counter. It was called the Devil Bar; its bright red carpet and strobe lights were beautiful but strained my eyes. Still, it was the best place for us to be until morning. It was then that I heard it. Coming from the counter was English.

I told Ren to stay at the table, but she had already rested her head on my bag for a nap. I shuffled over to the counter, sat on a bar stool beside the guys, then listened to their conversation. They were arguing about sports, and they spoke with an Irish accent. My presence didn't affect their conversation whatsoever. I realized one of the greatest things about being a foreigner—eavesdropping on other foreigners. The bartender noticed me, then asked me a question in Hungarian.

"Sorry. I American." The guys stopped their conversation then looked at me, stunned. The look on their faces was worth all the annoyances of that night, "One beer. Please." I pointed toward one of the logos on the fountain, then she nodded.

"You're American?" Said the Irishman on the left.

"Yep. Tennessee born and raised. What's yall's name?" The man on the right budded in,

"I'm Andrew, and his name is Ryan. We're from Ireland." The bartender handed me my drink, then I raised it,

"Well, it's a dream of mine to drink with the Irish. Cheers?" We clinked our glasses then began to talk. They were in Hungary on a business trip. What business they worked for, they didn't say, but it involved drones. They asked me what I was doing there; given they were also Englishmen, I trusted them. I told them of the journey, and my goal of making it to Ukraine. Their faces turned grave. They went silent then looked at each other.

"You're a brave man," Andrew stated, "I'm sure you'll do great." I brushed it off.

"Eh. I'm probably gonna die." I forced a chuckle. Their faces didn't change. I shifted the subject back to sports, and we discussed American football extensively.

"I don't understand the rules. It's so complicated," Ryan confessed. I then went on a ten minute explanation of the rules only to get confused looks. I needed more beer to explain, so when the bartender came back, I asked for another. She reached out her hand and said, 'Credit card.' I was confused, but obliged. She swiped it then handed it back.

"Thank you. Come again." I wasn't sure how 'Another' sounded like 'I'm done,' but I took it as a sign to leave. I started towards my bags when Ryan stated,

"Play us in foosball. There's a table right over there." I agreed, then we started to play. After several rounds of whooping our butts, Andrew was the grand victor. As he celebrated with a beer, I looked at the time as he chugged. It was almost 1:30, and I was about to collapse from exhaustion. I knew I wouldn't make it to the morning. It was either pass out in a random bar with strangers or find a place to sleep.

"Well, guys, I've got places to be. It was fun hanging out. It's been a while since I've gotten to kick back. If I survive the war, I'll let you know." I gave them both a handshake then picked up my bags, waking Ren up in the process.

"Wait," Andrew handed me a Hungarian coin, "In case they have foosball tables in Ukraine, maybe you can play." I nodded then put it in my pocket. We waved goodbye, then entered the deserted street. I still have that coin, but it's lost in a sea of other Hungarian change, and it's not going anywhere.

"Ren, I gotta make a decision fast. Should I find an alley for us to sleep in or take a taxi to the nearest forest?" I turned towards Ren, who was barely able to keep herself upright, "Damnit." I cursed, then lifted her onto my shoulders and pressed on. She fell asleep immediately; it was up to me to find a place for us to sleep. It was then I saw it. A large marble stone building with 'Hotel' written across. Everything inside me said this was the place we were looking for. I walked inside then went to the front desk.

I asked for a room, and for the first time that night, someone said there was one available. He asked me if I was sure, given how late it was, but I didn't care at that point. Ren was fast asleep, and I wasn't far behind her. I closed my eyes then swiped my credit card. I didn't want to know how much it was, and I still don't. After he gave us the key, we took the elevator to our room.

Once inside, I tucked Ren and Ruby into bed, then went to the bathroom to shower. While showering, I looked back on our night. It was a crazy night, and one of the most fun nights of my life. It made a smile grow on my face, thinking about how crazy my life had become. I wasn't bored anymore, and knew it would only get crazier from there. After showering, I went to bed then wondered what the next day would bring. Little did I know that the next day would make my night in Budapest seem normal.

7

ROAD TO THE BORDER

T he next morning, I woke up then stepped out onto the balcony to smoke. It was a completely different scene than the night before. With how crowded it was, you would have thought you'd woken up in a different city.

"Todays the day." I turned towards Ren, who had finally woken up.

"It's morning already?" She asked as she rubbed her eyes while yawning.

"We can't afford to sleep in. We've got a big day ahead of us." She leaped out of bed, fixed her hair in the mirror, then met me on the balcony. We gazed out into the city as I went over the plan with her. She'd heard it ten times by then, but listened without complaints. After finishing my cigarette, I showered, then changed into my all-black outfit. Once Ren finished getting ready, we went downstairs then ate our fill of the complimentary breakfast. It was good, aside from the wandering eyes. My outfit didn't help my military bag look any less suspicious.

I checked us out of the hotel, then we started down the busy street towards the train station. Upon arrival, I got our ticket and was shocked to see it had a departure time. After a short wait outside watching a man and his pet rat do tricks, we boarded our train with little difficulty. The only problem was finding our train car, but after a few guesses, we found the right one.

We went in then found our seats. It wasn't at all what I expected. It looked like the inside of an airplane, with more windows. Still, I was fascinated by the experience. Once our tickets were punched, the train took off, and my first train ride began. It wasn't as cool as the air train in New York, but it was still amazing to see the terrain of Hungary. Luckily for us, we had window seats, so we spent the whole ride gawking at the passing terrain and pointing out the best views.

It was a smooth ride to Nyíregyháza, but the trouble started when we got off the train. I didn't have an ounce of signal, and that was a problem. Without my phone, I was powerless, but good ol' free WiFi was my friend. I joined the train station's WiFi then loaded Google Maps. There were no taxis available on Bolt so we had to walk. I took screenshots of our route to the bus station, then we started walking west. We ventured west down the street, with my compass app as our guide, using every bit of free WiFi I could find to ensure we were on the right path.

It was tedious, but eventually, we found the bus station but realized something. We'd been in Hungary for almost a week, and had yet to try Hungarian food. It would've been insulting to leave without at least one meal. I led us to a nearby restaurant, which looked like an old cowboy saloon. We were the only people besides the waitress, her baby, the cook, and an old man I assumed to be the manager. It felt like a scene straight out of a movie. A stranger from a far-off land rolls into town, walks in, then asks for a meal. Only this was more awkward because I was involved.

The waitress sat us in a booth then took my order. I asked Ren what she thought we should get, but she smiled awkwardly. She'd never been to Hungary either. So I did what I always do when visiting a new place- I shifted the menu to the waitress and said,

"You. Pick. For me." I grew up poor, so you eat whatever is given to you. Even if the food is disgusting, you still eat because it's that or air. She nodded and took the menu. She asked what I wanted to drink, so I told her Coke. She returned a moment later with a glass bottle of Coke and a cup. She removed the cap, so I reached for the bottle, but she put her finger up.

"No. I pour." She poured the Coke into the glass then slid it towards me. This is a very normal thing across Europe. It might just be a Tennessee thing, but drinking from a glass Coke bottle is fancier than drinking from a glass cup. It also dirties a cup for no reason. I understand why they do it, but it just seems like a waste. I don't remember what I ordered besides the mushroom soup, but I remember it being perfect. After I paid and used the restroom, we returned to the bus station.

We walked inside after briefly stopping at a park bench for a smoke. I'd never used the bus before, but assumed I'd buy a ticket at the counter. We went to the desk, then I slid my phone under the glass, explaining how I wanted to go to Lónya. The man called over his daughter, who did her best to translate. She said no buses were available to Lónya. The farthest it would go would be a city called Mándok. It was okay in my books. It was another hiccup in the plan, because now it meant we needed to cross the Tisza River. But being in Mándok would allow us to build a raft to get across. I took a picture of our bus route on his screen. Our bus would be leaving in thirty minutes, the last one that day.

"Okay. I buy ticket then." I said while pulling out my

credit card, but he put his hand up to the glass. Using Google Translate, his daughter wrote,

"You pay driver. Cash." I nodded then pulled out a 100-dollar bill, American.

"Yes?" I asked. She shook her head.

"Hungarian." I nodded, pulled out my Google Maps, then typed in the closest money exchange. My eyes got wide as I saw that it was 20 minutes away on foot. I thanked them then we slowly walked out of the bus station. Once the doors closed, I took a deep breath. I turned left, then bolted down the street with Ren quick on my heels. All the while, cursing like a sailor.

"Peyty, I don't think we're gonna make it." Ren criticized me as she struggled to keep up with my pace.

"Not with that attitude. It's a twenty minute walk, so a ten minute sprint. That gives us a ten minute window. We can make it!" We sprinted through town and found the money exchange next to a mall. Luckily, there was nobody in line, so I got assisted immediately. To be safe, I converted two-hundred American into Hungarian, ending up with 72,000 forints. One dollar is worth 360 forints for those who can't do math. The thousands of dollars in my hand made my mouth water as I imagined, 'If only this was American.' In addition, I transferred 100 dollars into Euros just to be safe.

I thanked the woman, then we sprinted back towards the bus station, only we were more winded this time. But we returned to the bus station with five minutes to spare. We waited in line for boarding after asking a nice woman which bus was ours. Once we were in line, Ren and I collapsed on the ground, exhausted. We high-fived, then sat there until boarding started. Helpful tip when traveling- transfer your money as soon as possible. Once it was our turn to talk to the driver, I proudly flashed my bus route. The driver, however, kept a straight face.

"Where? Do you want to go?" he asked. I pointed at my phone, thinking there must have been a miscommunication, but he slowly pushed my phone away and repeated himself again.

"I want to go, Lónya." I stated, while pointing at my phone. We went back and forth for the next three minutes until he turned the other way. Ren leaned in and whispered,

"Maybe he doesn't understand you." I nodded, then looked back at the driver. His face had turned as red as a tomato, and he was banging his arms against the steering wheel. I turned towards Ren then grabbed her by the hand. We weren't getting anywhere, and an angry Hungarian in enemy territory wasn't what we needed. As we turned to walk off the bus, a man blocked our way. He was short, bald, plump, and wore a devilish smile.

"Excuse me, are you American?" He asked in perfect English. Beside him was a boy a little younger than me.

"Yeahhh." I thought his smile couldn't grow anymore, but I was wrong. It seemed to have grown twice in size, and he chuckled.

"I'm American, too. I'm originally from Hungary, but I go back and forth. Don't be scared. I'll help you. Where are you trying to go?" I explained how I wanted to go to Lónya, and after a glance at my bag, he nodded. He told me to get off the bus as he talked to the driver, so I did as he said. After speaking to the driver for a few minutes, he got off and gave me a curious look. He crossed his arms then grinned again.

"Don't be ashamed. Traveling as an American is hard, especially alone at your age. I got everything worked out, so don't worry. Lónya huh? Why are you going there?" He winked, so I knew we were safe. He's American, so he understands.

"I'm just going to visit my girlfriend. That's all." I winked back. He nodded, then we shook hands.

"Well, good luck with your 'girlfriend'. I'll be rooting for you. You should get on the bus before it leaves. I also got to say goodbye to my son." After thanking him for his help, Ren and I waved goodbye as we hopped onto the bus. The atmosphere of the bus had changed from before. It was quieter despite there being more people. Once on the top step, I looked out into the bus and saw that every eye, including the driver, was on me. When I looked at the driver he nodded, so I assumed that everything was settled. I grabbed Ren's hand, then we slowly walked down the aisle, watching as the eyes followed us to our seats. Once we plopped down, a tall blonde woman from the front of the bus came and sat beside me.

"Hello. Do not worry. We will take care of everything for you. We will get you to where you have to go." She handed me a piece of paper with instructions for my bus route then told me to wait. I sat back in my seat and did as she said. I had no choice but to put my faith in the people I was so scared of. It was a gamble, but one we had to take. All I could think was, *Have I had one bad experience with a Hungarian besides that man and woman in the airport?* My life was in their hands.

After thirty minutes of driving, the woman escorted me off the bus. She told me to wait and wished me luck. She hopped on the bus, then they drove away, leaving us in the middle of nowhere. We sat down on a bus bench, I lit a cigarette, then stared off into the distance.

"Do you think we can trust them, Ren? We're in enemy territory. If just one of them calls the police, then we're done. The police could be coming for us right now. They just wanted to get my guard down. We could just start walking now. They wouldn't be able to find us. We could get to the border by tomorrow." Ren didn't acknowledge my question. She kept looking forward as her little legs swung back and forth. She hummed a soft, happy song to herself, calming my nerves,

"Fine, I'll just have to trust them. But if we end up dead, well, I guess it's on me." I took a deep puff from my cigarette then closed my eyes. I heard the sound of a bus then dipped the cigarette in a nearby puddle. As it slowly came down the road towards us, I debated if we should leave, but that question was in my head, **What type of man do you want to be?** And the answer was a man that looks for the good in humanity. The bus came to a halt, then the doors opened. Ren swung off the bench, then we walked towards the door.

"Are you? The American?" The driver asked while pointing at me. I took a deep breath then smiled.

"Yes. I, the American." He nodded and waved for me to get on. Once we reached the top step, I pulled out my wallet to pay, but he shook his head and told me to sit down. I looked out onto the bus to find it empty. I was the only passenger on the bus besides Ren, of course. We sat in the front seat, and the bus went on.

For the next three hours, the bus drivers dropped me off and picked me up all over northern Hungary. Some of my rides had people on them, but most didn't. Not a single driver let me pay. After each ride, the drivers would either wish me luck or salute me. I'd give them my Luke Skywalker salute back, then they'd go on their way. It was truly a monumental moment. The entire bus company orchestrated a plan to get the American to where he needed to go, and it warms my heart every time I think about it. All I could think as we traveled closer toward Lónya was, *I'm not going to let them down; I'm going to save as many people as I can, so this wasn't all for nothing.*

It was 10 o'clock, and we were on a crowded bus. From my map, we were nearing Mándok, and from my calculations, we'd be able to get to Lónya in no time. Very soon,

We'd be approaching the next obstacle- crossing the border. But we'd still have a 6-hour walk first. As I stared at my phone, an elderly woman across the aisle was eyeing down my military bag. Eventually, we made eye contact, and after seeing my smile, she knew I was American. She pulled out her phone then typed a message.

"You American soldier, yes? What do you do in Hungary?" After seeing how supportive the Hungarian people were, I decided to trust her, and I didn't want to lie to an old woman. She reminded me of my memaw, and something about her told me I could trust her. I typed my response.

"I go to Ukraine to fight. I am not a soldier." When she read the message, she looked at me as if I were her own grandson. She offered me food and her house to stay in, but I declined. I had my sleeping bag, and intended to stay the night in the woods if needed. I explained how I was going to the border on foot, and she clicked her tongue.

"You need to talk to the police. They help you." The thought of talking to the police sent shivers down my spine, so I rejected her advice. She begged me to talk to the police, but I kept refusing, and she eventually shook her head. However, I knew from her eyes that she didn't accept it. Once we got to Mándok, my gut told me to stay and watch her. She pulled out her phone, and I saw as she typed, '112.' My heart immediately sank to the floor.

"Ren, we got to go NOW!" I picked her up and sprinted down the road. Up ahead, I saw a forest and knew we just needed to get to those trees to be safe. From there, we could hide out until the search was over. I ran no more than 2 minutes when the police sirens turned on behind us. I froze in my tracks then plopped Ren and my bags down. It was over. They'd seen me, and it's over if they ever see you. Ren and I raised our hands, and the cop car slowly pulled before us.

"What we gonna do?" Ren asked as she looked up at me with a worried expression.

"Well, we can either fight or talk our way out. Considering they have guns and I have a knife, we're gonna choose the ladder. But if it gets bad, we'll just do something stupid. You with me, Ren?" She nodded, then we slowly walked towards the police cruiser. The driver window lowered, revealing two male police officers inside.

"Passport. Please?" One of the officers asked. All I could think about was how screwed I was. *Why does it always end with cops?* All my life, police have been involved no matter how much I avoid them, and it would just get worse. The officers ran the numbers on my passport, talked for a moment, then called someone on their laptop. They spoke for 15 minutes, and the entire time, I was sweating bullets. Thoughts of me spending the rest of my life in a Hungarian prison littered my mind.

However, I didn't feel in danger. Despite being five feet away from the people I was avoiding, there wasn't any hostility coming from them. Still, I thought of taking my passport and sprinting into the woods, but knew it was a mistake. I decided to keep my trust in the Hungarians but had a backup plan. The officers eventually stopped talking with the man on the other line then handed me my passport. The officers waved for me to come closer, so I stuck my head inside the cruiser. The man on the other line began to speak, and it was English.

"Hello, is this Peyton?" A little surprised, it took me a second to respond.

"Yeah. This is he." Ren giggled at my response, and I gave her a light tap on the head.

"Yes. My name is Sergey. So, you do not want to go to Lónya. If you want go Ukraine, you must go Záhony. Look on screen." The officers pointed to their laptop, and it showed the route to Záhony. It was better than going to Lónya because we didn't need to cross the Tisza River, "You cross over by train. It be six-hour walk. You do it yourself. Okay?" I wouldn't have cared if he said six days, I wasn't going to jail.

"Yes, sir. I understand." I cheerfully replied.

`"Okay. Good luck." And with that, Sergey hung up. The officers wished me luck, waved goodbye, then drove off. We were alone in the middle of nowhere. The night was approaching, it was getting cold, and we had a 6-hour walk. Despite all that, I was the happiest man in the world. I picked up Ren and spun her around while chanting,

"I'm the luckiest man in the world!" I put her on my shoulders, loaded up our route to Záhony, then began our long walk to the border. Soon after the sun set; we were walking in the dark. Thankfully, it was a half-moon that night, so we were still able to see where we were going. I wasn't going to jail, and we'd be in Ukraine by the next day as long as we just walked. All I had to do was keep moving forward.

I managed to find signal to call my family members. I told them of my day, and how Ukraine was on the horizon. My dad was not very enthusiastic, but after asking me to turn around, he wished me luck. My grandmother on my mom's side was ecstatic, as was her lifelong friend Renae. They, like my mom and brother, understood why I was going, and were happy since I didn't get arrested. My grandmother didn't like me going, but she told me,

"Please just be as safe as possible and do good. I'll be praying for you. Please keep me in the loop." Unlike the rest of my friends and family, who already wrote me off as dead. Renae had a different response,

"Peyton, I don't agree with what you're doing, I don't like it, but you go kick those Russians' asses!" I thanked them for their support then kept walking. Ren and I hiked on through the countryside for the next few hours. At midnight, we snuck through a small subdivision. It was the only light for miles, so we were happy to see it. I wanted to stop and ask for water, but the dogs in the neighborhood detected my scent. As if all hell broke loose, every dog in the neighborhood began to bark, so we quickly ran through the neighborhood before everyone came out to see us.

After escaping, we walked up a large hill, then down into a dark forest. The trees were so tall they blocked all light from the moon, so I resorted to the light on my phone. I wasn't afraid, though. After everything I'd been through in the past few weeks, walking down a dark path in the forest wasn't so scary. I'd always feared the dark, but that fear was gone. Now, the darkness was a shield to hide us from our enemies. Ren didn't see it the same though. She walked closely with me, and stiffened with each russell from the bushes. After a few minutes, it began to mist, so we used my jacket as an umbrella. I considered making camp in the woods for the night, but something told me to keep going. We pushed on, and just a few minutes later, Ren stopped then pointed ahead.

"Look." She declared, then I saw what she was looking at. Up ahead were car lights bouncing off the top of the next hill. It was the first car lights we'd seen all night, and my gut told me it was for us. *Trust the Hungarians*, I told myself, *They haven't let you down yet*. I turned off my flashlight then we moved to the side of the road. I took Rider from my pocket and watched as the car slowed down. I looked at Ren.

"If things go south, we'll run into the forest. Got it?" I instructed. Ren nodded, then we stared at the car in front of us. It was a gray SUV, so I thought it was a family looking to help a hitchhiker, but I was wrong. The doors flung open, then four Hungarian military officers stepped out. One was tall, thin, with several colorful medals. With him were three young soldiers. Two men with rifles, and a woman with a green duffle bag. *Running is out of the question*, I thought. I dropped Rider, and we put our hands up. To top it all off, I gave my big, goofy smile, and the soldiers began to laugh.

"You. The American?" The Colonel asked. I nodded, then slowly handed him my passport. They must have never seen a US passport before, because each soldier took their time flipping through it. After the last soldier was done, he handed it back to the Colonel then went inside the vehicle.

"Empty. Bags," the female soldier ordered. I nodded then did as she said. I pulled everything out then handed it to the soldiers to examine. When I pulled out Ruby, the soldiers and Ren laughed, then my cheeks went red. They talked among themselves, and I assumed they said, 'Little American boy needs a doll to sleep with.' After finishing, they gave me a thumbs-up. The colonel called me to the car then patted me down before handing me a pen, paper, and cell phone with someone on the line. The man spoke; it was Sergey.

"Okay, Peyton. Write down father's and mother's names and numbers on paper. We need to know who call in case you die in Ukraine. Understand?" I was at a loss for words. The Hungarian military was helping me. I would have written down my social security number if it meant getting across the border.

After writing down everything they needed, they shoved my bags in the back of their SUV, then we squeezed into the car. I had to cram in the back with the guys while the girls sat up front with the Colonel. The Colonel changed gears, and with that, we were on our way to Záhony, going 50 miles an hour instead of 3. In no time, we were in Záhony. It was dark, much like Budapest. The only light came from their yellow light poles. It made it hard to see anything besides the road. The car stopped in front of a large prison-like building, and once again, doubt filled my mind. Ren looked behind me and smiled. She was right. I needed to trust them.

We got out of the car then got our bags from the trunk. We passed through a barbed wire fence then entered the facility. From the inside, it didn't seem like a prison; it was more like a police station. The only light was from a side building, where a man wearing a neon jacket waved for us to come in. Once inside, the soldiers brought us into a concrete room with wooden benches and lockers. We sat on one of the benches and I looked around for an escape route. However, the only way out was through the soldiers at the door or a metal door to the side. I stared at the wall, waiting for the next crazy thing to happen.

After 15 minutes, a man came in through the metal door. He wore a green sweater, black vest, and a brown fedora with a feather. He was tall and slender, and he looked to be no older than thirty. He put his hands in his pockets then slowly walked towards me. We locked eyes, and from his sincere look, I knew he wasn't the enemy.

"Nice to finally meet you, Peyton. I've been working all night to get you here. I'm Sergey, the man from phone." We shook hands, and we looked at each other again. His face had the same expression as my brother Drew's, "First off, please empty bags again. I'm sorry, but it precaution."

"I understand." I emptied my bag one piece after another. With each object, I showed it to the soldiers then placed it on the ground. All the while, Sergey asked me the typical questions like- What state are you from? What do you do? When I showed them my earplugs, the room erupted with laughter. One of the Hungarians said something that I assumed to have meant, 'At least he's prepared!' I sighed while pulling Ruby out, then got the expected laughs. After finishing and getting the okay, I packed it all back up.

"So, we are not going to hurt you. You can go to Ukraine

if you want. We are just curious. This is very strange. Not every day, young American come through Hungary to go to Ukraine. We just want to know why." I looked over at Ren, then at Sergey.

"Because it is the right thing to do. Innocent people are dying, and I won't stand by and do nothing." Sergey translated what I said to the soldiers, then one of them asked a question. Sergey nodded then asked me,

"You understand that you will die, yes?" I put my hands together while considering plan D.

"Yes. I understand." Sergey translated again, then the room went quiet. The only sound was Ren sneezing then wiping the snot on her dress. Sergey let out a long sigh then left the room. He returned a few minutes later with a bag of food and a case of water.

"Here. This is for your journey. I know you have food, but here is more. You need all the food you can get. Follow me; I will help you." I refused his gift, but he wouldn't take no for an answer. Ren and I then followed Sergey through the side door. We walked through a hall then outside to a pathway. It led to a large white tent with a blue and yellow flag hanging from its front flap. Behind the tent was a long, wired fence with a train behind it. It wasn't a prison or a police station- it was a train station. We walked inside a large concrete building with lion statues outside. It was empty inside except for a woman dressed in all-black leather waiting to buy a ticket. The woman made eye contact with Sergey then asked him a question. They talked briefly before turning to me.

"Peyton. What a. How you say it? Coincidence. This woman bought ticket to Ukraine but doesn't want it and wants sell it. You need buy ticket. You can buy it from her. You lucky." I handed her seven thousand forints, then she gave me her ticket. She thanked me then left the train station. I'm not sure if it truly was a coincidence, but I like to think it wasn't. Sergey brought us to the white tent then sat us at a table in the corner.

"This is Ukrainian refugee camp. They stay here until they find a place to go." For the first time, I saw what refugees looked like, and they weren't what I expected. When you think of a refugee, you picture a bony person in ragged clothes, but they just looked like ordinary people. They wore the same clothes as us, and you'd assume they were Americans if you didn't know any better. The only difference was the look on their faces. They all wore the same expression-despair.

Sergey told me to wait for my train, wished me luck, then left. I looked around the tent. There weren't more than twenty Ukrainians, but half were children. One was a teenage boy who couldn't have been older than 15. He wore an American Eagle hoodie with Nikes. From the look in his eye, he'd seen hell; I could only imagine what he saw. Ren and I were only there for a few minutes when a young man entered the tent. He locked eyes with me then stormed over. He sat across from me and put his hand out for a handshake.

"My name's Brian. I'm from Chicago. I just finished school, and I'm volunteerin' here. I gotta say, what the hell ya doin here man?" He went on a rant about me being young, inexperienced, and how I'd die a gruesome death at the hands of the Russians. Nothing I hadn't heard before. He also told me Americans are seen as 'Big Money'. I was already aware of it, so I brushed it off, a horrible mistake. After he was done, he left then returned with a hot meal. He wanted me to eat, but I refused, because I didn't want to take food away from the refugees.

"Quit bein' so stubborn, Peyton," He yelled as he buried his head in his hands. It was something I wished I could do, "I don't wanna see ya die man. Listen, you don't gotta go to Ukraine. You can stay here and help. You'll be more useful.

I'll give ya a few minutes to decide." With a tap on the table, he left to let me think. I looked down at my meal then at Ren. She'd rummaged her way into the bag of food Sergey gave us then found a candy bar. It made me smile to watch her pretend to feed it to Ruby then quickly stuff it in her mouth. I decided to eat my food and be a little less stubborn.

I weighed out each option even though the answer was obvious. I told my dad what was happening, and he told me to stay. I wish I could say my decision to go was solely based on my desire to help, but that would be a lie. All I could think about was everyone back home who was watching me. Each one thought, 'He's not going to make it. He's going to chicken out. He's not gonna survive.' We were right there on the border. I'd given up my entire life for this one chance and caused so much heartache. I couldn't stop. Not when I was so close to proving everyone wrong. I had to see it through to the end.

When Brian returned, I told him my answer, then he sighed. He told me the train would be leaving soon, so he escorted us to the waiting area. When we walked in, it was complete chaos. Hundreds of people were scrambling around trying to get everything situated before the ride. All of them were darker complexioned, unlike the pale people inside the tent. I didn't think anything of it. I'm American, so I assumed that everywhere else in Europe was just as diverse as us. We sat down against a wall to begin our wait for the train.

As we waited, I charged my phone at an outlet. Two children approached me after a few minutes. One was a girl around the age of Ren, and the other was a boy who looked to be about five. I set my translation to Ukrainian, but they didn't know how it worked. They changed it to Romanian instead then typed. They wanted to use my charger because their parent's phones were dead. I didn't see anything wrong with it. As their phones charged, I talked to the family and asked them what they needed. They said they needed food and water, so I gave them the bag Sergey gave us, however, they asked for more. I offered them my bag of food, but they said no.

"Money. I. Need. Money." The little boy cried. I couldn't say no to a child, obviously because of Ren, so I pulled out my wallet then handed him a 1 dollar bill. Like a swarm of vultures, the entire family flew down upon my wallet, and soon, I'd given a dollar to each family member. As I went to close my wallet, the two children began to cry; it felt like a spell had fallen upon me. I ended up giving away over 100 dollars, and only stopped because the announcement to board the train came over the intercom. Everyone rushed outside onto the platform and began to wait. Because the people were so short, I could see over the crowd and saw the train. To no one's surprise, it was brown and yellow. A blonde woman plucked me from the crowd, then escorted us across the tracks ahead of everyone.

"You are more important than the rest of THEM." She stated as we crossed the train tracks. I thought, at the time, that her comment was cruel to the Ukrainian people, but I'd soon realized what she meant. She put me in line to board the train. As we waited, I noticed that everyone in line was white. *Are they being racist,* I thought. Once it was my turn, the blonde woman spoke to the man, then he nodded. He punched my ticket, stamped my passport, then said,

"Good luck." Ren and I stepped onto the train then reached the first empty seats. After we got on, the rest of the crowd flooded the train. As everyone was getting situated, one of the women who was in front of us in line entered our train car. She was pale with long red dyed hair and brown eyes. She looked at me, smiled, then left the train car.

Once everyone was settled, the train car began to move. It

didn't run but a minute before it came to a stop. After everyone was off the train, we got up. I wanted to remember this moment. We slowly walked towards the exit, reached the final step, then I took a deep breath. With all the power in me, I leaped from the train, landed on the train tracks, and yelled,

"WHO'S USELESS NOW HUH?!" A rush of pride fell over me. It felt as if I'd just won the Super Bowl, and the pouring rain was my Gatorade shower. I turned towards Ren and watched as she leaped into my arms. I swung her around as we cheered in victory, then lifted her onto my shoulders. I felt like I'd conquered the world, although our journey had just begun.

8

CHOP

We ran across the train tracks then followed the crowd towards customs. We were in our first Ukrainian city- Chop. Because we got off last, it meant we were last in line. The line was long; it looked to be a repeat of the JFK Airport. It didn't bother me, though. I was on cloud 9, and it seemed like nothing could bring me down. I was unaware of how soon I'd hit the ground. To my surprise, the redheaded woman I saw on the train was in front of us. She was accompanied by an older woman who looked to be in her forties as well as a teenage girl. The redheaded woman turned behind to look at me, I smiled, then she started to speak. I said my usual line,

"I American." She and the other two women spun around in disbelief. Ren and I snickered at their stunned reactions. The look on their faces was priceless. I pulled out my translator then handed it to her. She typed away, gave me my phone back, and I saw that she changed the translation from Romanian to Ukrainian. The redhead woman was named Maria, and the teenage girl was her sister Verna. The older woman was their mother. They lived in Kyiv but fled to

Hungary once the war started. Maria explained how they were on the way to live with their friend Maxeem in the mountains of West Ukraine until the war was over. Naturally, they asked me what I was doing. Through google translate, I explained my goal to fight the Russians. Maria almost had a heart attack after she read it. She replied,

"That is stupid! You will die! Many friends I grew up with have died already. Do not fight!" I brushed it off by saying,

"I'm smart. I've got a plan. Don't worry." Along with a thumbs up. She rolled her eyes then dropped it. I told them about my journey and wanting to help the Ukrainian people. They were surprised that I could do it at just twenty years old. It would become a common reaction across my journey. After I finished, it must have been something I said, because Maria's eyes widened. She took my phone then wrote,

"You know these people are not Ukrainians? Ukrainians are white. They are not refugees. They are Gypsies. They travel from country to country and take free food from homeless shelters and refugee camps. They use their children to beg for money from travelers, and when they get old enough, they have children. The cycle continues." Just like that, my feet hit the ground. I had just been scammed, and I was furious. I'd heard of the stereotype of Gypsies, but never thought it was true. My euphoria from my recent victory was quickly overpowered, and I was filled with pure rage. I went silent. Maria noticed my mood shift then faced forward. Ren pulled on my arm and asked if I was okay, but I shoved her away. Her eyes got big, then she began to tear up. I rubbed my temple in frustration while saying,

"I'm sorry. I didn't mean it. Just leave me alone for a bit. Okay?" I wasn't in the mood to talk to anyone. We got up to the window then I handed the woman my passport. She stamped it then welcomed me to Ukraine. My anger was so hot that those important words I'd waited to hear for weeks did nothing for me. We took our first steps into the train station. I immediately noticed the color change. The train station had several gray columns, and the floor and ceiling were blueish-gray. I also saw the lack of seats. All the chairs were taken by the Gypsies, so all the Ukrainians were forced to sit on yoga mats in the corner. That sight sent me over the edge. The nerves in my forehead began to pop, and the slaps on my wrist weren't helping anymore. I had to get some air.

"Ren, don't follow me. Just wait here, okay?" She sheepishly nodded as I stormed out of the train station. I walked down a flight of stairs then sat down on an abandoned water fountain. All the lights were off around me, so the only light came from the train station's windows and my lighter. After lighting my cigarette, I took the longest puff of my life, then felt boulders of stress and anger roll off of me. Ren came outside then sat beside me. She didn't speak but just hummed a slow, sad song as I continued to smoke.

"I'm sorry I got mad. It wasn't right to take it out on you. It just makes me so mad, you know? I've given up everything to come here and help people and just got taken advantage of! It just makes it seem like it's all for nothing. As if my life is for nothing." I wanted to cry, but my body wouldn't let me. Ren stood then stepped in front of me. With her hands on her hips she proclaimed,

"You're my travel buddy, Peyty. I don't think your life is worth nothing. I'm sure everyone at home doesn't think that either. I think It's okay to be kind, but not too kind. Too much of anything is bad, and be kind to the right people. Some people don't deserve it." She said while waving a finger in my face. Sometimes, Ren could say exactly what I needed to hear. I patted her on the head then replied,

"Yeah, you're right. Thanks, Ren." I pulled her in for a hug. As we hugged, the doors to the train station opened. The mother and daughter of the family who scammed me walked out. The mother saw me, then pointed at me as if giving a command to a dog. Her daughter nodded then walked towards me. She reached her hand out and asked,

"Money?" Tears began to fill her eyes, but mine were already watering. I looked at Ren beside me, then the battle ensued in my head. *It's not her fault. She's just doing what she's told. If I gave all my money to this little girl she would have enough to last years. She could get away from this lifestyle and live a long, good life. But if I do, then I won't be able to help Ren.* I had to pick between the lives of two children, and it tore me apart inside. I looked down at Ren, and knew my answer. I shook my head at the little girl.

"No." I declared. The girl began to sob, and I pointed at my cigarette, "Smoke. Bad for you. Go away." The little girl shook her head back and forth while continuing to sob.

"Please! I hungry! Please, sir!" *This is war, Peyton. You have to be tough. It's the only way you'll survive. It's the only way to protect the free world. It's the only way to save Ren.* I swung my arms forward, then shouted,

"LEAVE! GO AWAY! GET OUT OF HERE!" The little girl cried into her hands, cursed me in her native language, then returned to the train station with her mother. Just like that, I refused to help a starving homeless child. I came all that way to save a child but ended up turning my back on one in the process. It's ironic, isn't it? Ren comforted me until I gained my composure. It was in the past. I chose to save Ren, so the only thing to do was to keep moving forward.

Now that my hourly heartbreak was over, it was time to continue the mission. We went to the counter inside to buy a ticket to Kyiv. Once there, I looked towards Maria and the other Ukrainians in the corner. They all stared at me as if waiting to see what I'd do next. I wanted to go to Kyiv, because that was how Plan D could work, but there weren't any trains available. The Russians had been in Kyiv for over a month at that point; it was deemed 'too dangerous' for citizens. The next best city to go to was Lviv. It was okay in my book, because all I needed to do was find a military base.

The worker typed my information into the system, and by a miracle, I wasn't flagged. She told me my ticket would be 700 Hroshi. Hroshi is the Ukrainian currency. I didn't have any, so I offered her my credit card. The woman shook her head. *Okay then. We'll do the global currency then,* I told myself. I pulled out a 100 dollar American bill, then she shook her head again. *Oh, come on! Fine. Hungarian it is.* I pulled out 10,000 forints, and again, was denied.

"Hungary is 500 feet that way, and you won't accept their currency?! If I was at the border of Mexico in Texas, I'm pretty sure they'd let me pay in pesos!" That is what I wanted to scream at the woman behind the glass. Instead, I sighed then pulled out my last option- Euros. And to nobody's surprise, she rejected those too. *What's the point of a European currency if you don't take it?* I screamed in my head. At the time, I was unaware that not all European countries use Euros. She told me I'd have to exchange my money, and after some googling, found out the nearest money exchange didn't open till nine. Another helpful tip when traveling- If possible, exchange your money before entering the country.

There was nothing for us to do but wait out the night, then try again after exchanging my money, or so I thought. As I was about to turn around and leave, a man approached me. He was tall and slender with a buzzed head. He looked to be a few years older than me, and struck a resemblance to a guy I'd gone to church with.

"My name Max. I pay for your ticket. No problem." This wasn't the Max that Maria was looking for to ease any confusion. Max put the money on the table, without asking for my consent, then the woman slid the ticket over. I gave him Euros in return, which was worthless to him, then he asked me to follow him. He led us over to the corner where the other Ukrainians were. Besides Maria and her family, there was a mother and her two young sons. After introducing myself, Max asked,

"We go to safe place until train. It has food and water. Okay?" Given that he'd just bought my ticket, I had no reason to not trust him. Besides, our other option was to stand outside the train station for the next few hours. I agreed, then we went outside. After a few minutes, two minivans pulled in front of the fountain, then we started to load our bags. Max spent several minutes trying to make everyone's bags fit. Eventually, he made it work with a good hard slam. We stuffed ourselves into the minivans, and like that, I'd gotten into a stranger's van with no clue who they were. Sorry, Dad.

We didn't drive long before we stopped in front of a small elementary school. It was a typical school besides the boarded-up windows and sandbag walls in front of the doors. I was reluctant to go in, but I was all in at that point. We walked inside, went down a hallway, then entered the cafeteria. Inside was a grown woman and a preteen girl. Upon seeing Max, the girl sprinted across the room then leaped into his arms. I assumed they were family.

"Uh. American. What your name?" Max asked. I'd told him earlier at the train station, but he'd forgotten.

"My name is Peyton." He knit his eyebrows.

"Pey? Ton? That name I never hear before. We have no 'Pey-Ton' in Ukraine. Well, we have food. Water. Please. Help yourself," Ren and I helped ourselves to their sandwiches and sat down at a table by ourselves. I was still hesitant, and the abandoned school didn't give me much confidence. The second we sat down, everyone migrated to our table, "So Pey-Ton. Why you here?" Max eagerly asked with a grin.

They didn't give me the option to be alone, but I'm grateful for it now.

I told Max my story, and he translated it to the rest with the best of his abilities. Here, I discovered one of the most fun games you can play when traveling the world- The English game. It's simple- you only speak English with the locals, and see if you can understand each other. Because English is the second language in many foreign countries, people view it the same way we view Spanish in America- I want to learn it, but it's too hard. The only difference in other countries is they feel more insecure about not knowing English because it's the universal language. Almost everyone who met me wanted to test their English, hence the English game.

The rules are simple- you start speaking normally then go down to meet their level. Everyone's English is ranked on a scale of 1-100. If someone is 1-10, they know almost no English. 10-40 are people who know basic words but still can't hold a conversation. 40-70 can hold a conversation, but only if you speak slowly and use simple words. 70-90 are those you can talk at normal speed and use more complex words. Anyone who is 90 or above is classified as, 'They could move to America, and nobody would know.'

On an English scale, Max was about 50. He could understand me if I spoke slowly without an accent. Every few lines though, he'd stop me then ask what certain words meant, such as 'Massacre' and 'cravings.' When he asked which state I was from, I told him Tennessee, then he looked at me dumbfounded. I wasn't surprised. Tennessee isn't the most well-known state, but at least we're not Iowa.

"Tennessee. Jack Daniel's whiskey." I told everyone, then they laughed while nodding. I asked how the war was going, so Max showed me a picture of the updated war map on his phone. A few days after I'd left, the Russians were kicked out of Kyiv, but most of east Ukraine was still under their control. He informed me of the major cities, such as Mariupol, Kharkiv, and Zaporizhia, that were under fire by the Russians. All that went through my mind as he spoke was, *Which one of those cities will I pick to go to?*

He asked what I knew about the war. I told him that in America, we knew about the Ghost of Kyiv and 'Russian warship, go F__ yourself.' For those who don't know, the Ghost of Kyiv is said to be a fighter pilot who took down over six Russian fighter jets on his own. Max explained that the Ghost of Kyiv is real, but nobody knows who it is. Some say it was a group of men, while most say it was only one. As for the warship, just look up what I just said on YouTube. You'll find a very cool video.

Max also gave me a history lesson on Ukraine. One that is long and complicated. For a broad overview, this is the story- Before Russia was the powerhouse it is today, it was first known as the Kyiv-Rus empire in modern Ukraine, the capital being Kyiv. After several years of growth, it spread across Europe and Asia, but what is now western Ukraine was taken over by Poland, including Kyiv, which it held for hundreds of years until Russia got it back in 1667. The rest of Ukraine was later conquered and held by Russia until the collapse of the Soviet Union in the 1990s. Despite being conquered several times, Ukraine held onto its own identity.

Because Ukraine was on the far left of the Russian Empire, it experienced all European wars. They experienced World War 1 and Hitler's invasion of Russia in World War 2. Hitler's invasion was incredibly brutal for the Ukrainian people because of their large Jewish population. They weren't safe from their own leaders either. During 1932-1933, Stalin sent a famine across Russia to subjugate his people, and one of the places hit the hardest was Ukraine. Ukraine was targeted because it was the breadbasket of

Europe, and Stalin wanted complete control. An average of 13% of Ukrainians died during the famine. Since the famine, Ukrainians had been cautious of Russian rule. When the Soviet Union collapsed in the 1990s, Ukraine voted for independence, but not really.

Their Presidents who were voted in, to no one's surprise, all happened to be pro-Russian. Despite achieving their freedom, they were still locked in a cage. It wasn't until 2014 that everything changed. The people were done with the corruption in Ukraine, as well as the extensive control from Russia. The people wanted a better country and better relations with the West. They protested in the streets, leading to several demonstrators being shot and killed. During the chaos, Russia invaded Dombas, starting the Russian-Ukrainian war. Since then, the Ukrainian people have become wary of their government and Russia. For the next eight years, the war in Donbas continued until Putin invaded the rest of Ukraine in 2022. This is a broad overview; I left out a lot of their history, but this is just the basics.

After the history lesson, Max shared Ukrainian music with me. I learned about their rally song for the war, 'Stefania' by Kalush. Kalush is Ukraine's Suicide Boys. The song is about how his mother is growing old and how he wants to hear her lullaby again, like when he was a child. Many Ukrainians associated his mother with Ukraine and the desire for her lullaby as freedom. I found it fascinating that a rap song was a war song. It shows how modern the war truly is.

He also showed me other popular war songs like 'Obemy' by Okean Elzy. If Kalush is their Suicide Boys, Okean Elzy is their Michael Jackson. I've gone through most of his songs, and each one he sings with enough passion to move mountains. He showed me another war song called, 'Bayraktar'. It's a Ukrainian military song dissing the Russians. In it, the subtitles wrote something strange.

"Max. What does Orc mean?" Several of the Ukrainians chuckled. Max filled me in once he got done laughing.

"Orc what we call Russian invaders. Russians are not bad people. But the Russians here. They monster. They can not be man. Man not do what Russians do here." I nodded then looked at Ren. She was staring blankly ahead at Max when her face lit up.

"Oh!" She reached into my bag then pulled out Ruby, "Peyty. Make Max hold her!" I looked down at Ruby then up at her. I knew exactly what she had in mind.

"Absolutely not." Ren's smile turned to a frown, then she stuffed Ruby back in my bag. She flopped her head on the table, then looked up at me with puppy dog eyes, "Okay. Fine." I pulled Ruby back out, then offered her to Max. He smiled awkwardly at me as he grabbed Ruby.

"Look Peyty! Its-"

"Max and Ruby. I know." Ren erupted with laughter. We all talked for several hours about the war, America, and life. It was my first time speaking with Ukrainians, and I learned how friendly they were. They welcomed me with open arms and treated me as an ally. It was there that I first experienced the family of Ukraine. When it came time, I said my good-byes to everyone, then we walked with Maria and her family to the train station. It was still early, so we went to the side-walks and used our phones' flashlights to guide us. Once we reached the train station, we found seats inside and waited for our train. All of the Gypsies had left. In the meantime, Maria and I talked through Google Translate. She tried to teach me Ukrainian but only managed to get through the basics.

"Yah is I. Ti is you. Me is we." At 'me is we', I knew that Ukrainian would be one of the hardest things I'd ever learn.

Ren encouraged me, but her 'You got this!' didn't give me much confidence. After the 10th failure, Maria decided to change the subject. She typed on her phone and asked me a question I'll never forget.

"Why do you want to die?" It seemed like a stupid question. *I'm doing all of this to avoid dying,* I thought while typing my response,

"I don't want to die. I just want to help people. If there is a chance I could save someone's life. A child. Then it is worth trying." She read my message then shook her head. She put her thumb to her lips then typed,

"You want to save people. You would rather die than not save someone. I understand, but if you die in the process, then why does it matter? You are young with much life ahead. **Everyone dies one day. If it is a child or adult.**" I looked down at Ren, nuzzled in my arms. She looked up then giggled. Maria had a point. Everyone dies someday, but I went the opposite way with it.

"If everyone dies someday, then it doesn't matter if I die now or fifty years from now. My life doesn't matter. The only thing that matters is that child's life and the free world." Maria groaned then turned red in the face. In a fury she typed, then shoved it in my face,

"You are so stubborn! Stop trying to die! Come with me. We are going to the mountains to live with my friend Max. There, we will live until the end of the war. You do not have to die. You can live." Her request moved me. A stranger, a beautiful woman, was asking me to come with her to live in the mountains. I'd be lying if I said I didn't consider it. I could start a new life in the mountains; say goodbye to everything. However, I couldn't turn my back on Ren. Not after what happened earlier with the Gypsy girl. I'd come so far and given up too much to turn back. It was Ren and I against the world.

"Sorry, but I have to do this. I have to go to Kyiv. See this through. Thank you." Maria gave up, but she wasn't happy. We exchanged Instagrams to keep in contact, then soon after that, our train started to board. We were in different train cars because I waited so long to buy my ticket. Maria hugged me tightly when we got to our train car then wished me luck. I said goodbye to them, then Ren and I boarded the train.

This train was how I expected trains to be. It was almost identical to the Hogwarts Express, but it was navy blue instead of crimson red. I quickly found our cabin because even I couldn't mess up counting. It was smaller than expected. Inside were two cushioned benches with a table by the window. On top of the benches were pull-down lofts. Besides Ren and I, there was an elderly woman who looked longingly out the window. As soon as I sat down, I felt my body change. It felt like a giant black hole was inside my stomach, except this wasn't hunger. It was a feeling I'd never felt before, and as the train began to move, my body felt weaker and weaker.

"What's wrong?" Ren asked. I began to tremble more and more. I didn't have the strength to speak. I had no idea what was going on. *Am I sick? Did I contract a disease from being in Europe?* I was freaking out. I laid out on our bench, and my eyes shut on their own. No matter how much I tried to force them open, they wouldn't budge. Ren beat on my chest and screamed for me to get up, but it was useless. There was nothing I could do besides hope I'd wake up eventually.

For what felt like an eternity, I laid there comatosed. Every bump on the train tracks raddled me; I wished with each one that it would kickstart my body again. I repeated over and over in my head, *Don't die, you'd come too far to die like this.* It was one of the scariest moments of my life. I didn't know if I was dead or alive. Three hours later, as if God resurrected me, I sprung up in control of my body again. Ren sat up, leaped onto me, and cried,

"I thought you were dead!" I rubbed her head to calm her down. I wasn't sure what happened, but I was grateful to be alive. The feeling inside my stomach was gone, and my body was back to normal. To this day, I'm not sure what it was, but my best guess is that it was exhaustion. Because I was in constant fight mode for over 24 hours, the stress and fatigue on my body had built to the max. Once I was finally somewhere safe, my body knew it could rest, so it was going to take it whether I liked it or not.

"It's okay. I'm not dead yet." I looked out the window to see we were going up the west mountain range of Ukraine, the Carpathian Mountains. My eyes moved to the elderly woman; she was crying. It bothered me to see her upset, so after gaining my composure, we began to talk through Google Translate. She informed me that her husband, brother, and two sons were fighting in the war. It made sense why she was upset. The chances of all four of them coming back alive were slim to none. She had left the country and was returning home.

"What's the point of being alive if everyone I love is dead?" She wrote, and there wasn't much to disagree about. I steered the conversation away from the war, so we talked about America for a while before my body began to shut down again. There wasn't much I could do. I told her I was going to sleep, then control over my body disappeared as quickly as it returned.

"It's okay, Ren. I just gotta sleep for a bit. Just watch over my body for a while, okay?" She nodded; it felt good to see she wasn't as upset as before. My body shut off, and once again, I was comatosed. I laid motionless as the train pressed towards Lviv. My fear wasn't as great this time, but I was still defenseless. Thankfully, nobody tried anything, then four hours later, I had control over my body again. The woman was gone, and Ren was sitting at the end of the bench watching me.

I checked the map and saw that we were almost halfway to Lviv. I wasn't aware of how slow trains are. There was a time skip in every movie and it made sense now. For the next 8 hours, Ren and I did everything we could to ease our boredom. We watched out the window at the passing terrain, hoping to see carnage from the war. Since it was western Ukraine, there wasn't much to see, but the view was breathtaking. We played what games we could on my phone, but without WiFi, we could only use puzzle apps. It got old fast. We settled on dancing to music and relaxing. I had no idea what Lviv was like, and throughout history, being relaxed has never been a problem.

9

LVIV

A fter an uneventful train ride, we made it to Lviv. As the train slowly came to a stop, my phone began to work, and I was already looking for my first destination- a money exchange. My number one priority was to exchange my cash for Hroshi, and as soon as we were free, we leaped off the train then started our hunt. Once we were out of the train station, I stopped and looked out into the city. Because it was a rainy day, the clouds covered the skies, turning the city gray. Their gothic buildings and color choice also didn't help brighten the mood. Like the train station in Chop, most buildings were green, gray, or dark blue.

The refugee center beside the train station didn't help with the tone either. The Red Cross had roped off a street offering food, medicine, and clothes to people passing through. The lines wrapped around the block as families waited in the rain for relief. One of the first things I noticed was that everyone was very pale, making me the darkest person there. Everyone also had similar facial features that made mine stick out. For the first time, I was a minority, which felt interesting.

I pulled my hood over my head, then we marched down the busy city street. It was weird not hearing English at least once. Whenever someone opened their mouth, I would start to listen just to hear what sounded like gibberish. It was like I was in a parallel world, making me feel even more alone than before. I put my earbuds in to ease my anxiety. If I couldn't hear everyone speaking a different language, I could assume everyone spoke English.

I hurried my way through the crowds towards the money exchange. With each person I almost hit, I smiled then saw them give me a look of disgust. I remembered that smiling isn't normal in Europe. Still, I continued and got dozens of nasty looks before managing to make myself stop. *Just look depressed,* I told myself as we ventured through the crowds, *Just show how you actually feel.*

We reached the nearest money exchange inside a shopping mall, then I converted 1,000 dollars into Hroshi. One US dollar is worth about 33 Hroshi. The GDP in Ukraine is similar to Budapest's, and from my time traveling, I noticed how cheap everything was. To put it into perspective, a large 2 liter of coke at a convenience store was around 50 Hroshi, and this was in wartime. Paying for food was never a problem.

I was blown away by their money. It didn't feel real, because it was colorful like monopoly money. The 1 dollar bills were blue and yellow like the flag and smaller than the rest. 5's were blue, 10's were pink, 20's were green, 50's were red, 200's were purple, and 500's were orange. Just like our money, they have former leaders on their bills. In addition, though, they have famous poets, painters, and civil rights activists.

"What's the plan now?" Ren asked as we ventured down the street. The rain was pouring more now, but luckily, almost every building had a canopy.

"I've got a job to do- find the Ukrainian military. There I can ask to join. The real question is- Where is it?" As soon as the words left my mouth, I spotted it across the street like a miracle from God. It was a tall green building with a large sandbag wall around its perimeter. In front of the sandbag wall were dozens of large metal jacks, Czech hedgehogs as they are officially called. To top off their defenses, two Ukrainian soldiers were at attention with AK-47s.

"Well, Ren, diplomacy has worked so far. Might as well ride it as far as it can go." Ren gave me a thumbs up, then we ran across the street to the military base. Once we were in sight of the guards, they fixed their eyes on me. We stopped, I dropped my bags, then we lifted our hands. We slowly walked closer to the soldiers while watching as they gripped their rifles in anticipation of my next move. I smiled and said,

"Yah Americano, Peyton Robinson. Yah here to help. Take me to your leader." I slowly handed the soldiers my passport then watched as their faces turned from confused, to shocked, then back to confused. One of the soldiers went inside then returned with their sergeant. He was a tall, stoic, slender man with short gray hair. He looked me up and down then fixated on my military bag.

"Military?" He asked as he pointed to my bag. I shook my head. He nodded then ordered his soldiers to frisk me and search my bag. I assume because that's what followed. After they were done, they forced my hands down then motioned for me to come inside. Once inside, the sergeant took off upstairs but left one guard to watch me. I tried to avoid the awkwardness, so I looked around. The room was rather empty aside from the crates of supplies, war maps, and several rolls of chicken wire. It was dusty, not from age, but from sawdust. A few minutes later, a soldier in glasses walked down the stairs. As we shook hands, I noticed that he was taller than me, a rare occurrence.

"I'm Sergey. Nice to meet you. What are you doing here?" He asked bluntly. I figured it was a given.

"I want to join the military. I can join the foreign legion or the Ukrainian army. I'll go anywhere, you say. I'm just here to help." He nodded then sized me up. His face reeked of curiosity but also sorrow.

"Hold on. I'm making a phone call." He left then came back a few minutes later with his sergeant. "I made a phone call. I just need to ask a few questions. How old are you?" He took out a pen and paper then began to write.

"I'm twenty." He slowly shook his head.

"You must be 25 to fight. Are you soldier from USA?" I replied back,

"No. I am a college student, but I learn fast." He scribbled on his paper then asked his next question.

"Do you speak Russian or Ukrainian?" I gave the biggest smile manageable paired with a thumbs down,

"Nope! Not a lick, but I'll learn." He shook his head,

"I see you wear glasses. They do not allow foreigners with glasses. It causes problems." He said while wearing glasses,

"I have contacts. No glasses needed." Sergey said that having contacts still disqualified me. Out of all the reasons to disqualify someone, the contacts qualification seemed the most idiotic. He scribbled down my response, put the paper into his coat pocket, then looked at his commanding officer while sighing. He looked me dead in the eyes; I saw the pity emanating from them. It made my anger flare, but nothing compared to what he said next,

"I'm sorry. We cannot use you. You have no qualifications to help us. **The best thing you can do is go home. You'll be more useful there.**" The words struck like daggers. I looked over at Ren in disbelief. She was just as shocked as me. He'd said the same thing everyone had told me, but he did it with pity as if I was weak. In addition, it meant that Plan B was up in smoke, so it was now time for Plan C- almost certain death. They'd just dug my grave, and I would fall in. I was so scared my legs wouldn't move. Ren noticed, grabbed my arm, and pulled me towards the door.

"Come on, Peyty. Let's go. There's no point being here anymore." She was right, no matter how much I wanted her to be wrong. I thanked them for their time, then we rushed

out of the military base. Once out of sight, we rested on a wet park bench, then I lit a cigarette while staring open-eyed at the busy road. I was like a deer in headlights.

"It's okay, Peyty. You would have been a great soldier if they gave you a chance. Let's go get something to eat. I saw a Domino's on the way here. I'm starving!" Ren's attempt to cheer me up didn't help. My mind was focused on those words, 'The best thing you can do is go home. You'll be more useful there.' It felt like it was me against the entire world. The world thought I was weak, and I wanted to prove them all wrong. I just wanted the chance to save someone.

"Ren, I've come so far! I've given up so much, and they still don't want me. I've given my soul to this, and they just casted it aside. Maybe everyone back home was right. Maybe I am useless. Everyone there believes it, and everyone here believes it, too. If the whole world thinks I'm worthless, then maybe I am." Ren slapped me across the face. Her little hand didn't hurt much, but did what it needed to do.

"Peyty, you're not useless. The fact that we're here means you're not. You're brave, Peyty. That's the best part of a soldier. You're not useless; you just don't see your use yet." I rubbed my cheek then looked up at the sky. I took a deep breath, slapped my wrist with my rubber band, then released all my frustration.

"You're right, Ren. I'll just have to show them. I guess I'll just do Plan C-run into the battlefield alone, empty-handed, with no experience. Fine! Whatever! I'll do it on my own. Come on, Ren. Let's get something to eat." I lifted Ren onto my shoulders then walked down the street, singing and dancing as we went. I didn't care anymore about the wandering eyes. My chances of surviving the war were just cut in half, but all I could think was, *If you go from 2% to 1%, is there really any difference?*

We went to a Domino's nearby, but it was so crowded that there was nowhere to sit. In addition, their screen said it would take an hour of waiting, so we decided to try somewhere else. After walking a few blocks, Ren dragged me into a small cafe. It wasn't as crowded as the Domino's, but there still wasn't a place to sit. The waitress introduced herself then said in English that the place was full. I shrugged my shoulders then we headed for the door, but someone who I assumed to be the manager yelled,

"Is that. Your bag?" She pointed at my military bag. I nodded, then she rushed us over to a reserved table. I protested, then attempted to stand up, but she forced me down. She wouldn't take no for an answer. I figured it wouldn't be a problem if we ate fast, but a few minutes after we sat down, the couple who had reserved the table came in. After a long conversation with the manager, the couple nodded and stood patiently at the door. Everyone in the cafe had heard the conversation, went quiet, then stared at me. Even the chefs in the back came out to watch.

"Ren. Sometimes I hate you, and this is one of them." Ren only giggled as my face turned as red as a tomato. The irony of being denied becoming a soldier and then getting soldier treatment was God putting the icing on the cake to my terrible day. It was the most awkward restaurant experience of my life. When I tell you that I devoured my food as quickly as possible, I mean it. I inhaled it as soon as it came, left a tip, then went to pay for our food. The person who spoke the best English checked me out, and once it was over, I apologized to the couple then we shuffled out of the cafe.

By the time we got out, it was beginning to get dark. I needed time to think about my next move and was far too exhausted to travel. I found a cheap hotel nearby, then asked for a room. The hotel was old, dark, and resembled a castle. Once we reached our room, we collapsed onto the bed then sighed. It had only been two days since we'd slept on a bed, but it felt like weeks. I took a long-deserved shower then began to plan our next move. After brushing my teeth then changing clothes, I sat down with Ren.

"Alright. Let's look at the map. We're here in Lviv. We need to get to Kyiv. Because it's the capital, it'll be the country's nervous center. If we can get there, we should be able to find a ride to the red zone. All we gotta do is get there." Ren nodded in agreement, then we discussed our options. We tried to look up train rides to Kyiv, but none were available on the website. The next option was a lift to the city, but that would take much convincing to the driver. There would also be the 'I could die' charge, and I wasn't comfortable paying it. The Hungarian and Ukrainian people had been very nice, but I still wasn't very trusting. I had a puny knife on me and a pocket full of cash. Hitchhiking was off the table, so it meant one thing.

"I guess I'll walk to Kyiv. It says it'll take a 7-day walk to get there. Given my long legs, and I stayed on the highway, I could reach Kyiv in 2 weeks if I walked at a normal pace." Ren looked at me as if I was insane.

"Are we seriously going to walk 336 miles? Have you ever done that before?" I rubbed her head, put my hand to my heart, then exclaimed,

"It may take a while, but with enough determination, it's possible! We just gotta put our minds to it. Besides, I could use the cardio." The weeks of binge eating were going to come in handy. After deciding on our route, I turned on Disney Plus but it was blocked. I tried HBO, Hulu, and Paramount Plus, but they were blocked too. The only apps that worked were YouTube and Netflix. I turned on YouTube, then Ren and I watched Max and Ruby, per her request, until we fell asleep.

The next morning, we checked out of the hotel. After checking out, we stood around to use the free WiFi to load my map, when I overheard the man at the counter speaking English. I was so excited I rushed over to the man and asked,

"Do you speak English?!" The man looked at me with a cold expression.

"Yeah. What about it?" I was so excited. I hadn't been able to talk to anyone the day before and wanted to speak so badly. I had Ren to talk to, sure, but I wanted to talk to someone new.

"I'm American!" I cheerfully exclaimed. The man grabbed his bags, looked down at his phone, and replied,

"Good for you." He turned away then walked out of the hotel. At the time, I was distraught, but looking back, I understand. If a stranger approached you overly excited to talk, you'd be hesitant, too. Still, I just wanted to talk to someone, if only for a moment. I needed to stock up before leaving, so we stopped at a small convenience store. I bought a large 4 gallon jug of water, deli meats, chips, a cookie and cream fudge bar for me, and a drumstick for Ren. I've always valued rewarding myself for accomplishments, and my journey east had been tedious. After paying, we found a nice bench in the park where we could eat our ice cream. I made sure we took as long as possible to eat because as soon as we were done, it was back on the road.

While we ate, we 'people watched' as my memaw calls it. I noticed that a lot of them were women and children. Very rarely, we'd see a man, but if we did, they were elderly. One thing they all had in common was the lack of smiles. I'd make eye contact with some and smile, but they'd pick up their pace.

"Ren, I know Europeans don't smile at strangers, but this is so weird. What do they do instead?" Ren bit into the cone then smeared the melted chocolate across her face. It gave me goosebumps. I've always been a clean freak.

"They just look at each other. No reason to smile." She replied matter of factly.

"How do they know I'm not a threat then?" She giggled, finished her cone, and used her dress as a napkin.

"You don't attack them? Geez Peyty. You sure are dense. It's a MIRACLE you got us this far." I gave her a light punch in the arm, and her cry gave me an ounce of joy. I finished my ice cream then sprung to my feet.

"Alrighty. No more procrastinating. We've got work to do." We needed to reach the city's outskirts, so I ordered a taxi. It was difficult to find when it arrived because the traffic was terrible for one, and two, I don't know cars. I've never been a car person. The only thing that matters to me is if it can get me from point A to point B. I understand why people like cars; I just don't care for them. However, I wish I did when I needed to find my driver. I had no service, so I couldn't google what he was driving, and the dozens of cars around me made it more challenging. I resorted to going to every pulled-over car in my vicinity before finding my driver.

I set my drop-off point at the city's outskirts on Highway E-40. I found it funny because in Tennessee, we have I-40 highway that goes east to west. Fun fact: I-40 goes from Wilmington, North Carolina, to Los Angeles, California. The driver spoke a little English, so we talked about the war. He informed me that Lviv hadn't been affected much. The

Russians launched two missiles into the two tallest buildings in the city, and he pointed it out from a distance. The tips of the buildings were charred black, and bits of it had fallen off, but the rest was intact. He told me that the Russians had hit Kyiv hard; it made sense why the trains were down.

He parked on the side of the road then asked if it was the right spot. I gave a thumbs up, then we got out before he could protest. He drove back into Lviv, and I looked back at the city. We didn't spend much time in Lviv, but I promised we'd come back and properly explore it one day. I turned, and we started down E-40. I didn't take into account how much supplies I was carrying. I had my 50-pound military bag, a 10-pound bag of food, and a 40-pound jug of water. *Just man it out,* I told myself as we walked down the highway. I'd like you to guess how long before I had to stop for a break. If you guessed half a mile, you were correct. I collapsed onto the gravel and dropped all my weight onto the muddy grass. As I tried to catch my breath, Ren stood inches from my ear screaming,

"Is that all you got Peyty?!" I took one big breath, loaded up all my stuff, then started to walk again. *Only three hundred and thirty-four miles left.* The thought made me want to puke. Ren and I walked until we saw a bridge a quarter mile ahead. Underneath it were sandbag walls, metal spikes, and a lone soldier standing at attention. It was hard to see the soldier, but all I knew was that I didn't want to take any chances. To our right was a side road, so we took it instead. It led to several tiny run down houses with gardens and farm animals roaming in the front yard.

We went further down then crossed over a blown-up train track. Underneath the train track was a river, so we took our time traversing the rubble we used as stepping stones. We finally made it across then walked till we were past the bridge. I looked back to see the lone soldier wasn't a soldier, but a scarecrow. Ren busted out laughing, and I flicked her on the forehead. The scarecrow did its job.

"That's two today, Peyty. Not good." As irritated as her comment made me, she had a point. We weren't even two miles into the journey, and I was exhausted. I could have abandoned the water, but my military bag would still be torturous. I finally accepted there was no way we could walk to Kyiv. We'd have to catch a ride.

I looked on Google Maps then saw that the nearest gas station was a few miles up the road; it was one I was familiar with- A Shell gas station. After a thirty minute walk, we made it to the Shell. Once we made it to the sidewalk, we collapsed. I smoked while looking out at our possible rides. There were only three cars there. Two were pumping gas, and the other was parked to the side. There weren't a lot of options, but anything would be better than walking. I typed my message on Google Translate,

"I am an American trying to go to Kyiv. If you are going East, can I ride with you? I will pay." I stood and waited as people came by. The first man read my message then shook his head. The second man didn't even acknowledge me as he walked inside. I thought we'd stand outside that gas station for hours, but I was wrong. A tall bearded man with several piercings hopped out of the car parked to the side. He had a short black beard, and wore a denim jacket. He stood there watching me for several minutes while talking to a woman in the car. I tried not to make eye contact, but something about him felt familiar. The man walked over to me then looked down at my phone. He read the message, pointed to his chest, then said,

"Bro. I speak English. My name's Andie, whatcha need, man?" In perfect English. I was completely blown away. For a moment, I didn't know what to say.

"Uh my name's Peyton. I'm American. I'm trying to get to

Kyiv to fight the Russians. Can you give me a ride?" His eyes lit up. He shook my hand frantically as if there was no time to lose.

"Hold on, man. Imma go get a coffee. You want a coffee?" I shook my head, "Imma get ya a coffee anyway." When he returned, he handed me a cup of coffee then walked towards his car. He spoke to the woman in the car, then gestured for me to come over. I looked down at Ren. She shrugged her shoulders. She was thinking the same thing I was-*He speaks perfect English. He can't be too bad.* He introduced us to the woman in the car. Her name was Roksa, his wife, and to my surprise, she also spoke perfect English. In the backseat was their one-year-old daughter. Andie began to call someone, and Roksa filled me in.

"He's calling the train station. There should be a train for Kyiv." Andie got off the phone, put his hands on his hips, and exhaled.

"So, there is a train for Kyiv. There's two actually. One leaves at 18:00, and the other in twenty minutes, we gotta go now!" I nodded, and we all flopped into the car, then Andie put it in gear, "I've lived in Lviv my whole life. I know all the back roads. Don't worry, bro." We turned right then flew down an old gravel road towards Lviv. I'm sorry again, Dad. I got in another stranger's car; still didn't get any candy.

"So why couldn't I see anything online?" I asked as we bumped up and down from the potholes. He shifted the gear higher then swerved to the right, nearly hitting a fallen tree.

"Well, any normal person wouldn't go to Kyiv right now with the Russians, so they didn't bother to put it online. But you're the exception." I looked in the backseat. Roksa and Ren were holding tightly to the baby seat. Roksa smiled at me while giving a thumbs-up. From that alone, I knew they'd had a lot of experience with Americans.

"So, how did y'all learn English? Y'all speak so well." Andie and Roksa chuckled as he spun the steering wheel with all his might to make a right turn. Andie replied,

"I majored in business in college. That's where we met. English is the universal language, so if you learn business, you gotta learn English. Most degrees in college require you to learn English. Doctor, engineer, stuff like that. I also minored in English. But growing up, I was obsessed with Western culture. I watched Revenge of the Sith when it came out, and was upset that I couldn't understand it. Yeah, I had the voice over, but it's not the same. From that day, I vowed to learn English to enjoy everything America had to offer. I work for an American company at home, so that's also why. I told Ro when I saw you, 'He's not from around here. He looks American.' You just have that American stance." The part about me standing out didn't boost my confidence, but I felt more relaxed.

We talked about Marvel, Disney, and Star Wars for the next few minutes. He told me how popular Star Wars is; it was heartwarming to think of its impact worldwide. Because he spoke perfect English, I asked him questions about Ukraine and got good answers. He told me how Ukraine voted for independence in 1991, and how the country had changed since then. People like him had grown up in a free country and gained a new identity as Ukrainian, while the older generations identified as Russian. The new generation, like himself, grew up with western culture so they don't want to let it go.

"Ukrainians don't want to give up their connection to the West and America. Putin doesn't want Ukraine to affiliate with y'all because he wants to keep Russia closed off from the rest of the world. Our fathers and grandfathers told us of life under Russian rule, and we don't wanna go back to it. We wanna be our own country and have connections with the West and with Russia. That's why he invaded in 2014 and why he's continuing his invasion now," The car began slowing down, and I looked to see that we were driving toward a military stop, "Don't worry, we know how to handle these. Just don't talk. They'll have too many questions." Andie stopped, then a soldier came to his window. The soldier ducked his head inside, looked at the baby, then gave a thumbs-up. Andie thanked him, then we drove on as if we never stopped. Andie and Roksa laughed, so I looked at them, confused. Roksa explained after they stopped laughing,

"It's one of the perks of having a baby. We do it all the time. They just look at you and think, 'It's just a family. They're not a threat.' You won't BELIEVE how many places are available when you have a baby." *Duly noted,* I thought. When we got to the train station, we found ourselves in a car line with soldiers checking each one. My watch showed we had five minutes until the train left. While we waited, I thought now was the best time to ask this question,

"I appreciate y'all doing this for me, but why would you help a stranger?" Andie looked at me as if I was stupid, and rightfully so. Ren and Roksa giggled in the back seat.

"Why would you help us? You left your home to come help complete strangers. I should be the one asking you. Why are you doing it?" I put my hands together then watched as a soldier walked towards Andie's window.

"Because it's the right thing to do; that's all the reason you need." Andie nodded then rolled down his window. The soldier asked to see our passports, but after some convincing from Andie involving, 'We're late for our train. Look at the baby,' the soldier gave us the okay to drive on. Once Andie found an open parking spot, we leaped out of the car except for Roksa and their baby.

"Peyton, are you good to run?" I gave a thumbs up, and after a quick goodbye to Roksa, we began our sprint through the train station. I looked at my watch as we jumped down the stairs then slid around the corner. We had two minutes left to catch the train. Ren was slowing down, so I picked her up and threw her over my shoulder. We had to catch this train or lose 6 hours of valuable time. We ran down the tunnel then up the stairs to the platforms. To our right was our blue and yellow ride to Kyiv. Its engine began to roar while a short blonde woman wearing an all-blue uniform began to shut the doors on the train. Andie told me to wait as he spoke to her. After several minutes of talking, he called me over. The woman walked towards one of the train cars then opened a door as Andie and I spoke.

"What was that about?" I asked while pointing towards the woman.

"She was just curious why anyone would wanna go to Kyiv. I just told her you were American. You've got a train to catch Peyton," We shook hands, "Thank you for what you're doing for my country. It was an honor to help you out. Whatever you plan to do, I wish you the best. Stay safe." He gave me his Instagram, then we hopped onto the train. I gave my two-finger wave to him, as we went inside the train car. It was empty, so we were able to choose our cabin. Shortly after, our train began to move, and we were on our way to Kyiv.

"Ren, I can't believe it. In no time, we'll be-" Like lightning, the black hole in my stomach returned. My knees felt like jelly, and I collapsed onto the bench. Ren rushed to my side, but she wasn't crying this time. She looked worried, so I gave her a pat on the head and told her to protect me until I woke up. She nodded, then I lost consciousness.

A few hours later, I regained control of my body. With Rider in my hand and Ren by my side, we ventured through each cabin to see if we were still alone. After finding nobody, I went to the in-between of the train cars to smoke while Ren went back to our cabin. I tried to look at Google Maps but had no signal. There was no way to know where we were, and that thought made me happy. It felt as if I was on a magical train taking me away to a new world. To a new life. In just a couple of hours, we'd be in Kyiv and one step closer to my goal.

10

KYIV

We first stopped in the city of Rivne. I could see it because being in the city gave me enough signal for my phone to work. There, we picked up a few passengers. None of them stayed in our car though. From there, we headed west towards the city of Lutsk, then went south to Ternopil. I got off the train, stretched my legs, and enjoyed a restroom that wasn't going 50 miles an hour. Let's just say I found out pissing on a train ain't easy.

Before we departed, a volunteer group came on the train to hand out bags of food. The man wouldn't take no for an answer, so I accepted it. Inside were snacks of all different kinds. I didn't think I was deserving, but it was eat or throw it away. Ren sat across from me, and we devoured the bag of food until there were only crumbs. After eating, I looked at my phone to see we were finally on the way to Kyiv.

A few hours later, the door to our train car opened. Someone was coming in. My hand went straight to Rider, and I went to the corner of our cabin. A shirtless middle-aged man nudged his head in our doorway then began speaking. He wasn't wearing shoes or a shirt, and his pants were dirty. He asked me a question while pointing at his phone, but I shook my head then used my phone to translate. From several feet away, I could smell the alcohol on his breath, so my awareness rose.

We went back and forth, and he explained how he needed to charge his phone. I didn't want to waste more power on my battery than needed, but I came to help the Ukrainian people. If it meant charging a phone, then it meant charging a phone. He was so overjoyed that he hugged me aggressively. I offered him water, and he gratefully accepted it with cupped hands. I poured it into his hands then he drank without complaint. He asked me to wait a moment, then he returned with a cup he found in the trash. I poured his cup full, he thanked me, then left.

Pride swelled over me, because just like that, my goal was complete. I went to Ukraine and did something with my own hands. Even though it was just giving water to a drunk man, it was more than I'd have done back in America. The entire trip was worth it; I laid back on my bed while smiling. The engine's roar grew louder as I imagined what else I could do.

Ren let out a long yawn, and I was right there with her. The sun was beginning to set, so there was no point in staying awake. We had no clue what Kyiv would be like. For all we knew, Russians would be waiting for us at the train station. We needed all the energy we could get. Ren settled on the bed across from me; I gave her the camping pillow and my jacket to use as a blanket. I made do with my sweatpants for a pillow. She clung tightly to Ruby as she wished me goodnight, then we went to sleep.

If you've ever tried to sleep on a train, you'll know that it's nearly impossible. The engine roared like a lullaby, but the rumbles of the tracks inevitably woke us back up. I resorted to good old music. I listened to one of my favorite songs on repeat 'Touch the Sky' by Hillsong United, as we closed in on Kyiv. It reminded me of the long drives with my Dad to church. I'd think about how we'd jam to it together in silence as we drove down those curvy and bumpy roads. What I loved about it the most was its lyrics, "My heart beating, my soul breathing, I found my life when I laid it down. Upward falling, spirit soaring. I touch the sky when my knees hit the ground." All I could imagine when I heard the lyrics was me reaching out to Ren and everyone in need, and I was getting closer to saving them every second.

The man would return for water and snacks every few hours. He got so drunk he could barely stand, and after that, he never came back. I checked my map and saw that Kyiv was less than an hour away, so I decided to stay awake to not be caught off guard. I did push-ups, drank plenty of water, and ate a few granola bars. I also went ahead and had my morning cigarette and toilet time. We were about to enter a battlefield, so it was time to get serious. Once the train started to slow down, Ren finally woke up.

"Bout time. We'll be gettin' there soon." I told her while stretching. I packed up everything then changed into my all-black outfit. It was still night time; we needed all the advantages we could get. However, there was one major problem. My rechargeable battery was completely dead. To make matters worse, because of all the music I played, my phone was at 5%. *Not to worry. I just have to find a charging port once we get out,* I told myself, *In the middle of a war zone.* I smacked my forehead repeatedly while using the last of my battery to check a message on Instagram. It was from Maria.

"I talked to my friend Max about you. He has a house in Kyiv. He says he wants to help you. He says you can stay in his house. This is the address. He talks to neighbors. They let you in." I was so happy I could have died. I had no idea what we were walking into, what we'd do, or where we'd sleep.

Like a miracle from God, we had a safe place to stay. All I had to do was get us there.

"Ren, we've got our first mission. We gotta get to Max's house. All we gotta do is just not die. Easy peasy, right?" Ren wasn't paying attention though. Lights, for the first time in hours, shined into our train car. Ren was staring out the window in awe, so I went to see what she was looking at. She was looking at the beginning of our new life.

We could see the highways, well, what was left of them. Every few meters were bomb explosions, rubber tire walls, or hedgehogs. What was even more noticeable were the large splats of dried blood scattered along the roads. There were no dead bodies visible, which was a good sign, but the blown-up tanks and scorch marks were not. I couldn't tell who the tanks belonged to, but it didn't matter. It was a battlefield; a place where hundreds of men, women, and children once laid dead. It was a lot to take in, but I was mentally prepared. *Whatever trauma you get, you'll just deal with it when the war is over. You've got a job to do.* As the train began to slow down, I turned to Ren and said,

"The Russians should be gone, but they might not be, so we gotta keep our heads low. We gotta get to Max's house. There, we can fortify. Got it?" Ren slowly nodded her head. She didn't take the splattered blood as well as I did.

"What we gonna do if we see a bad guy Peyty?" Her eyes were wide with fear. We needed to keep hope alive, so I patted her on the head then said,

"I'll figure it out. I'm smart. I've managed to travel thousands of miles and three countries to get here. I've gotten us this far. It'll be okay, come here." As we hugged I could feel her body shivering, but it wasn't from the cold. I tried my best to keep my own shivering undetectable. Of course I was scared, but being scared wouldn't get us to safety.

When the train finally stopped, I picked up my bags then

we headed for the door, using what little energy left on my phone as a flashlight. Ren held my hand as we slowly walked down the steps and hopped onto the platform. We were finally in Kyiv, but it was so dark that we couldn't see two feet in front of us. Not to mention, it was so cold that it made us shiver even more. Thankfully, there were other people on the train. From my count, there were five. We walked over and joined the group. With a soldier escort, we walked into the train station through a dark tunnel.

After some walking, we saw a light at the end of the tunnel. We walked toward it, and it led us into the main lobby of the train station. It looked like a ballroom. Its large pillars rose to the sky, and its granite floor shined from the few candles on the chandelier above. Its dancers, however, were dozens of fully armed soldiers and refugees scattered along the walls, all too sad to move let alone dance.

I wanted to leave this sad dance, but there was no way we could go without my phone charged. I scoured the walls for an outlet, but all were taken except for one. It was in the corner next to an elderly woman sitting in a chair. It was ripped out of the wall, wrapped in duct tape, and looked to have been chewed on by mice. It was our only hope, though. I crossed my fingers and prayed to God for it to work. When I saw those green bars on my phone, I turned to Ren and gave her a high five. I also plugged in my battery, then sat on the cold tile floor. I wanted to use the cover of night to get to Max's house, but there wasn't a choice. We'd have to wait.

For the next two hours, we waited for my phone to charge. There wasn't much to do but sit against the wall and stare into the ballroom. I looked up at the closed-down staircase that led to the second floor, and saw two long banners. It was a sign I recognized. It was a sign for a nearby KFC restaurant. I took a picture to make sure I wasn't imagining things. I laughed while thinking, *They're fighting for their right to eat KFC.*

At 7:45, my phone was completely charged, and the sun was beginning to rise. It still wasn't dusk, but there was enough light to see. I grabbed my bags, then we stepped outside. Outside was another long tunnel with two elderly women walking down it. I remembered one of the rules of traveling- when in doubt, follow the crowd. I followed the elderly women, and we came to a steep staircase. After walking down the steps, I looked up to see the women struggling to get their bags down the stairs. I was supposed to keep my head down, but I came to help the Ukrainian people. If it meant carrying a bag, then it meant carrying a bag. As I helped them with their bags, I didn't say a word to avoid raising suspicion, then we walked into the city.

The city was worse than I imagined. Every building in sight was either scorched, torn apart, or completely leveled. Aside from the soldiers at the end of each street, there wasn't a person in sight. My map told me we needed to head west, so we started down the street. As we walked, we made sure to stay a few feet away from the buildings. Each building was boarded up with plywood, with the glass from their windows on the ground. Some of the glass was swept up in piles next to pushed-over trash cans, but most were scattered along the sidewalk.

In the middle of the streets were Czech hedgehogs, blown-up cars, cinder block walls, and chicken wire fences. Now and then, a car would snake through the barriers, but not without a stop from soldiers. Stores were blown open, and their insides gutted. The only thing left were dusty shelves that were set ablaze. At the end of each street were tiny bunkers made of couches, refrigerators, sandbags, tires, and a Ukrainian flag that flew in the wind. Occasionally there would be a posted sign that when translated means, 'F__ Putin.'

We crossed a few streets then started to walk uphill toward an apartment complex when alarms began to blare. They sounded like tornado alarms; only these were much louder. There was no doubt they were air raid alarms. I grabbed Ren by the arm and rushed her down an alleyway. We hid behind a pair of chard trash cans, then I sheltered her with my body as the alarms grew louder. Like lightning, something exploded far away, and it raddled the city. I covered Ren's ears to protect from the blasts and my cursing. *God, if this is how I go, so be it, but please don't let it be,* I prayed. We held on to each other, thinking it would be our last moments alive. Then, a few seconds later, everything went silent.

"Holy crap. We're alive!" I leaped up as we cheered at our survival, "Damn Russians." It was there I found out how getting bombed feels- getting bombed sucks. I gave a finger to the sky, then we continued up the hill faster than before. As we walked, we passed by other civilians, all were elderly with grave expressions. I smiled at each one, but most ignored me. It didn't bother me though. We just had our first life-or-death experience in war, and we'd only been there two hours.

After I had a much-deserved smoke break, we continued towards Max's house. To reach his house, we had to cross through an apartment complex with a playground outside. It was almost unrecognizable. Trenches were dug across the middle, and dirt hills were scattered across its body. Tank tracks had killed all vegetation and knocked over the swing sets that were now crushed to pieces. A garden for children had turned into a bloody battlefield for adults. *So much destruction, so much death, for what? Men, women, and children died for what? Land. Money. Power?* I thought about my friends and family, of my nieces and nephews, and how so easily someone could come in and kill them all.

We followed the directions to a subdivision then stopped when it said we arrived. A tall metal green fence in front of his house stopped us from entering. I texted Max on Instagram that I arrived, but with it so early, I knew it would be a while before he saw it. For now, we had to sit and wait. We slumped against the fence while we took a nap. I woke to two elderly men hovering over me in blue and white striped shirts.

"Що ти тут робиш?" One of the men said in a strict voice. I wasn't sure what he asked, but I knew it was a question involving me.

"Yah Americano. I know Max. Maxeem? Man who. Live here." I pointed towards the house behind us. The two men looked at me confused, so I translated it to them,

"I am a friend of Max. I was told to talk to his neighbor for a key to the house. Can you help?" The two men read my message for a minute before giving me a thumbs-up. One pulled out his phone then made a call, while the other watched me intensely. A few minutes later, the door to one of the fences opened, and a short, elderly woman walked out. She took one look at my goofy smile then sighed. She went back inside and came back with keys in her hand. She shooed the two men away, then unlocked Max's fence.

Inside was a yellow house, but we walked to the backside. Max's house was a duplex. In the backyard was a storage building and a tree house. The woman unlocked the door, handed me the key, then left. I looked at Ren, then at the open door.

"Follow my lead." I whispered while pulling Rider out, then turning it backwards in my hand.

"I gotchu, Peyty." Ren picked up a random stick, then we entered the house. To the left was the bathroom, and after some quick snooping, found it secure. We walked ahead then entered the kitchen. It was small but cozy. Along one of the walls was a hand-painted drawing of a black cat climbing a tree. In the kitchen was another door. I thought it was a pantry, but after opening it, discovered it was the toilet room. It was so small that the sink was directly above the toilet. Whoever thought of putting the toilet room in the kitchen is either a genius or should never design houses.

We slowly walked up a winding white staircase. As we did, we looked at the picture frames. Most were drawings, but some showed Max and his family. Max was married and had two daughters. From the pictures, they looked to be eight and five. They looked happy in the picture frame, but it was busted and laid in pieces on the floor.

On the second floor, along the left slide of the wall, were five doors. The first one was a playroom. There were stuffed animals, Legos, dolls, and a table and chair for a child. On the table were drawings—drawings I recognized. They were pictures of SpongeBob and his friends. I smiled as I flipped through them. I remembered when in school we'd draw pictures like that.

The second room was a girl's room that was cleaned out except for the papers on the floor. Even the mattress to the bed was gone. The only thing left was a painting of Pikachu on the wall. It brought me back to my childhood. I loved Pokemon as a kid. We moved on to the third room. Its double doors were wide open, so we hopped into view to surprise anyone. It was a living room. There was a couch, two dressers, a desk, and a long beige rug. Along the walls was a long, beautiful window that showed the city. In the corner was another door, so Ren and I slowly walked toward it. I took a deep breath, swung the door open, then thrust my knife into the doorway to only find air. It was an extra room full of junk.

We went towards the next room; it was the parent's bedroom. It had the typical stuff- dressers, book shelves, a bed, and an oven. Yes, you read that right. The oven was in the master bedroom. It was one of the biggest mysteries of my journey. The room led out to a balcony, but after a quick look, I found it was collapsing, so we returned to the hallway. On the way to the last room, we passed by a shrine to Jesus. It had several candles, charms, and beads on its shelf. Being from the heart of Tennessee, I'd never seen a shrine before and found it interesting.

At last, we were in front of the final room. The door was smaller than the rest, with a red skull and crossbones painted on it. I turned to Ren then gave her a thumbs-up. I opened the door quickly then stepped back. I wasn't met with anything except a little girls' room. I figured it had to have belonged to the youngest girl because the bed was for a small child. Make-up, dolls, and stuffed animals littered the ground. I looked up at the back wall then saw the window. It was covered up, but not with wood. The little girl had used her own stuffed animals to protect herself from the invaders. I collapsed onto the ground while cackling to myself.

"What is it, Peyty? Did I miss something?" Ren said as she moved into my view to get my attention. I kept laughing as I looked at the stuffed animals on the windowsill.

"It's just, you can't make this stuff up you know? It's just so sad. God, I bet you're laughing at me right now." I wiped the tears from my eyes then pulled Ren in for a hug, "She's not dead. She's not dead." Ren kept quiet until I finally managed to pull myself together. I slapped my wrist with my rubber band, then we walked back to the living room. I shut the door behind us and told myself it didn't exist. Max called me on Instagram a few minutes later. To my surprise, he spoke English,

"Hello? This Pey. Ton? This Max."

"Yes, this is Peyton," I replied.

"Okay. My neighbor told me you were inside, so I decided to call. You need to turn on the electricity and water. Do not drink water. It make you sick. Go to the panel in hallway." He led me through the instructions to turn everything on. When we were done, I thanked him for letting me stay. All he said was, "We're not using it. Maria says she trusts you, and I trust Maria. You come to help us, and the least I can do is help you. Can you send pictures? My family like to know how our house is." I agreed, and with that, he hung up the phone. He didn't ask any more questions. He let a complete stranger from a foreign country stay in his home without even seeing his face.

I hadn't taken a bath since Lviv, so I took one. When the faucet turned on, I was surprised to see brown water come out. Once the tub was full, it looked like a pot of soup, if the vegetables were bits of rust. It looked like the water I'd seen in videos about Flint, only now I was face to face with it. I stepped into the tub then hit my head on the ceiling. Like with some of the rooms upstairs, I was too tall. There was no soap, so I improvised with Dawn dish soap for my body wash. After an awkward cold shower, I dried myself off with my dirty sweatshirt then placed it on the electric drying rack. The iron from the water made my skin sticky, but it didn't matter to me. I had a bath, a house for protection, and a quiet place to sleep. We were dodging missiles earlier, so I was just grateful to be alive.

The air raid alarms began again, so Ren and I stayed downstairs in the kitchen until it was over. Once the attack was over, we went upstairs to the living room. I decided it would be our living quarters, and had good reasons. It had enough room for all my things, it was the only room that could lock, and most of all, it was the warmest. It was directly above the water heater, so its warmth could be felt through the carpet. It was cold even with all my clothes, so the little warmth from the water heater was a blessing.

"Alright Ren. We've got work to do," I sat down on my sleeping bag and Ren sat on the couch, "We're onto plan C. We've gotta get to the battlefield. We could try walking, but we saw how far that got us."

"Yeah. You quit like a loser." I tossed my head pillow at her then continued.

"Anyway, we need a ride. We need connections. Going alone to the red zone ain't a good idea. I'm stupid, but I'm not dumb. We need a group to go with. While we look for a ride, we might as well help here in the city. Back in Lviv there was a volunteer center outside the train station. We should go back and see who's there. You on board?" She nodded, then we left for the train station. There was just one problem- the gate door.

Locking the house door wasn't hard; it took a good shove with a quick turn of the lock. The gate door, on the other hand, was a different story. It was a traditional lock, so when the key went in, it had to be turned at the precise moment. If you pushed the key in too far it wouldn't budge. Even when it was at the right depth, it would still turn, but not enough. The air raid alarms started again, but I wouldn't move.

"I'll rather die than let this damn door win." I told myself. After thirty minutes of trying to lock the door and cursing, I let the door win. It hurt my pride to leave it unlocked, but it was clear that there was no winning that battle. I'd have better chances with the Russians.

More people were walking around than before, but it was nothing compared to the train station. It was a completely different atmosphere than before. Over fifty people were standing and running around the common area outside. There were over a dozen soldiers around the perimeter, each looking out for anything suspicious.

As we walked inside, we were stopped by a young soldier. Once he saw my passport he bursted out laughing. He called over two other soldiers, and all three chuckled as they compared my passport picture to my face. After they calmed down, they stared at me, waiting for a response.

"Peyty, I think they want you to talk." Ren whispered. *Welp, this or a bullet,* I concluded. I cleared my voice then prepared the most southern voice possible,

"Hello, ma names Peyton James Robinson. I come from Tennessee, an I'm here to kill all them Russians. Point me in tha right direction an I'll get er done!" I delivered it with a smile and a thumbs up. From the look in their eyes they had no idea what I said, but that was the point. They handed me my passport and allowed me to enter.

It was pure chaos inside. Hundreds of people were running in every direction, shouting and pointing towards the wall of departure times. I looked in the back and saw the restroom. I wanted to get my business done before getting down to business. I told Ren to wait, then I walked to the restroom. Between the men's and women's was a woman behind a glass panel. To enter the men's, you had to enter through a turnstile. Confused, I went up to the woman, then she pointed at a sign. You had to pay to use the restroom. Crazy right? I gave her one Hroshi, then she gave me my change. I went inside to a stall to find a squatting toilet. I decided I'd wait till we got home.

I wasn't sure where to go, so I went to the help desk. It was four older women wearing blue vests with 'volunteer' written on the back. I walked up to the table then told them I wanted to help. One of the women behind the desk stood and told me to follow her. She led us through a large fancy white door to another ballroom. Inside, There was a long wooden wall concealing the rest of the room. The only way to enter was through an open crack guarded by two soldiers.

The woman said 'American', then the soldiers stepped closer to examine me.

After they looked me up and down, they paused and looked into my eyes. I wasn't sure how different things were in Ukraine, but I knew the look they were giving me- an ego check. When men size each other up, they look into each other's eyes to see how they react. The eyes tell a lot about a person, and how you react to eye contact says even more. Where I come from, you look him dead in the eye and say, 'Do your worst.' but with your eyes. You're not there to start a fight, but you're not scared to have one. If you don't, he won't respect you, and that's what I did. After a few seconds, the soldiers nodded, I nodded back, then they let us walk through.

We walked through the crack and entered a volunteer center. To the right were dozens of men, women, and children working on military nets. They took a long piece of chicken wire, tossed it over a wooden beam, and tied strips of clothing onto it in bows. Further down were a handful of people hauling crate after crate of food, water, and medical supplies through an exit door into oncoming vehicles. In the middle of the room was a tiny closed-down coffee shop with a table and chairs in front. Sitting at the table were two men- a young bearded man and a middle-aged soldier. We walked up to the table, and the woman left without a word. As she walked away, the bearded man stood and started to speak Ukrainian, but I shook my head.

"Sorry. Yah American." The soldier at the table looked over in a flash. The bearded man looked at me in disbelief, smiled, then said,

"You're American? I'm British!" He spoke with a strong British accent. I jumped around with excitement,

"Oh my God, I thought I'd be alone! Give me a hug, my

English brother," We hugged and laughed maniacally, "What are you doing here?"

"Defending the free world! What about you?" He replied.

"Same here! I'm not gonna let freedom die!" He shook my hand as we continued to laugh.

"Do you need a coffee? I'll get you a coffee. How do you like it? Name's Ben, by the way. Yours?"

"Peyton. I take it black." He snickered then disappeared behind the coffee shop. He returned a few minutes later with a cup for each of us. Ren sat in the chair next to me then looked up with a smile. I knew what she was saying, 'You're with your people.'

"Nice to meet you Peyton, ma names Ryan, from Wales," The soldier said in a British accent, "Good to see another one of us here. It's been me and Ben here for a while."

"I'm so happy to see y'all. I thought I'd be the only one here." Ben and Ryan laughed while sipping their coffee.

"There's loads of foreigners here to help. People like us that understand what this war means. People back home, they don't see it." Ryan replied. He studied me for a moment then asked, "How old are you?"

"I'm twenty. Exactly! This war will decide the fate of the free world. There's no way I'm missin' it!" Ben spit some of his coffee out then shouted,

"You're twenty?! And you came here on your own? Have you ever traveled before?" He asked.

"Nope. I ain't even left my state in years." Ben exhaled and continued,

"You've got some balls. I'm twenty-seven, he's forty, but you're twenty? Geez mate. How was the journey?" I told them of my journey so far. From leaving my family, to Budapest, to being rejected by the army in Lviv. Ben told me that the same thing happened to him when he arrived; it made me feel better knowing it wasn't just me. Once I was done, they looked at me in disbelief. Ryan chimed in,

"Not everyone could do what ya did. Most people alive couldn't do that. When I was leaving, I went to everyone in my town and said, 'I'm flying my plane to Ukraine to go fight. Anyone who wants to come, I'll be leaving Saturday.' Over thirty men approached me and said, 'I'll go fight those Russians! I'll be there.' When Saturday came, do ya know how many people showed up? Two. You should be proud of whatcha did." It was one of the best compliments of my life. This soldier was calling me brave when he should've called me stupid.

"Well, the hardest part ain't over. I still need to get to the battlefield. You don't happen to be going out there, do ya?" I asked with a smile, but Ryan shook his head.

"Sorry, kid, I mean, Peyton. I've been fighting for the past month. I'm leaving this week for Wales to stock up on supplies, see my wife, and take a breather. I could talk to the Legion for ya, but it'll be pointless. They won't accept ya. You'll have to figure it out on your own." It was as I thought. I was going to have to do it on my own. Well, with Ren. After we talked for a bit, Ben brought me to the military net, and we got to work. We worked on the net while talking about our lives and of home. He didn't know of Tennessee, but he knew of Jack Daniels. Once lunch came, he said there was a nice bakery down the street. I wasn't willing to give up a chance to speak English or eat a donut. Ben escorted us to the bakery and we purchased some sweets. On the way back, we kept talking,

"So Peyton Robinson," Ben always used my full name, "You said you're from Tennessee, but where in Tennessee?" He pulled out a cigarette and offered me one. After the day I had, I couldn't refuse.

"Preciate it. I'm from Lebanon. It's near our capital-

Nashville. Home of country music." He cupped his hands, created a fire with his lighter, then we lit our cigarettes.

"Lebanon? Like the country?" He asked.

"Nah. It's named after Lebanon. We pronounce it- Leb-a-nen. Not Leb-a-non. Everyone gets it wrong. We also have another major city called Memphis. We have a sayin' in Tennessee- if you wanna get shot, go to Memphis."

"Interesting. I'm just from London. Born and raised. By the way, I like the way you speak. Your southern accent is relaxing to hear." I thought he was joking, but he was dead serious.

"Thank you. I like your accent, too." I noticed he walked with a limp. I tried not to make it obvious, but he caught me staring.

"Aw. This. I just got it recently. Here's a bit of advice- don't go out past curfew. You're assumed to be a Russian spy on sight. Curfew is 7 to 1900. Or 7 pm for you. Did you know about that?" I shook my head, "Yeah, I didn't either. It's not something that's talked about. It's just kinda assumed. I didn't know that when I first arrived. I was walking about after curfew, and these two soldiers spotted me. They came up to me then proceeded to beat the living daylights out of me. They ended up breaking my leg."

"Geez mate." I thought about that morning. If my phone wasn't dead then I'd be walking with a limp, or worse.

"I yelled at them, 'I'm British, I'm not Russian!' But they didn't care. I was compliant the entire time, but they kept beating me. They took my passport, saw I was foreign, then beat me more. They locked me in jail, saying my pants were 'Too Russian.' Whatever the hell that means. After a background check and a call to Britain, I was released. You know what they told me? 'Don't be out past curfew next time.' Then shoved me out of the station." He spit on the ground then walked faster. The thought of the experience was making his face start to turn red.

"I'm sorry, Ben. That's awful." He exhaled while flicking the ashes off his cigarette.

"It's okay. I understand. Anyone can be a spy. There are spies in the city right now. Someone willing to take a few pictures for some money. That's another thing- no pictures. I almost got thrown in jail for that, too, if the soldier wasn't so nice. Things are different in war. You'll have to understand that if you're going to survive. You're gonna need these, but you're already on it." He pointed at his cigarette.

"Yeah. I didn't smoke before, but now I have to. It's like-" The air raid alarms turned on, then Ren and I quickly sprinted towards an open alley. After finding a position behind a crate, I looked up to see Ben standing on the side-walk, laughing.

"It's clear you haven't been here long. It doesn't matter if you try to hide. It's literally Russian roulette! There's nothing you can do. It's an act of God. The only thing you can do is hope it's not you, and enjoy what could be the last minute of your life." It reminded me of what I told all my friends and family- I either die here a boy, or possibly die there a man. *And a man dies on his feet.* We stood up, then walked over to Ben. I picked up my cigarette, and we smiled at each other.

"Well, let's face death like men, then." We both looked up at the sky, waiting for our ticket to the afterlife. The explosions went off, the city shook, then the air raid stopped. We both gave a sigh of relief.

"Well, Peyton Robinson, we made it another round. That is why I smoke. I only smoke in war zones. If I could die at any minute, what does black lung matter?" I turned towards Ren. She was humming a melody to herself; when she noticed me, she gave a thumbs up. She was letting me make a new friend. We finished our cigarettes then tossed them into a trash can. I turned to Ben and asked,

"Have you ever had to PAY to use the restroom before?" He looked at me with a dead expression then said,

"Never in my damn life. It is so weird here." We laughed all the way to the train station. We returned to work on the net, and I told Ben how I wanted to find a job. He nodded, left, then returned with a man wearing a purple suit.

"Pey-Ton. Follow me. I help you." The man said. We exited the volunteer area then went upstairs towards a Kiosk. It was a phone carrier called Kyiv Star. He explained that being in Ukraine would require a new phone chip. With a new phone chip came a new number. Almost everybody uses Kyiv Star in Ukraine, which is very handy. You download their app and send money to your phone number to have it activated for so long. Every day, it charges you instead of every month. You can also pay for other people's phones as well. All you do is send money to their number.

After setting up my phone, we walked into another large ballroom. Inside were boxes of supplies, a soldier, and a woman typing frantically on her phone. As we walked up to her, she turned towards us. She was an older woman with long, shiny brown hair. She looked to be in her late thirties. She wore a large puffy coat with a blue volunteer vest over it. Around her neck were a pair of reading glasses, and a long gold cross necklace. The man introduced me to her, then she put her phone away. We locked eyes, and I felt something weird inside. I felt as if I'd known her for my entire life. As if she was someone I was always supposed to meet.

"You are American, yes? What is your name?" She talked in a soft but stern voice. She sounded stressed, as if she had the weight of the world on top of her, a feeling I understood.

"I'm Peyton Robinson. From Tennessee. I come to help. I

will do whatever you ask." She typed away on her phone, sighed, then put it away again.

"My name is Svetlana. Nice to meet you. Yes. There is a job that needs to be done. We need a person to dig graves. It is very hard. Can you do it?" In my head, I imagined the work. Long hours in the graveyard digging holes for funerals. I knew it would be hard, but it was exactly what I wanted. I assured her I could do it, then she said something I'll never forget. She asked me,

"It is hard to hold the head of burned dead child. Can you do it?" I wasn't expecting something so dark. I looked down at Ren beside me. *Could I handle that? No. I have to handle this. This is war, and this is just how war is. I can do anything I put my mind to.* I told myself, *Besides. You're just digging graves. You'll see the dead people in the caskets.*

"Yes. I can." Svetlana gave a weak smile.

"Okay. Make sure to take lots of pictures," She put her hand up to her eye then made a clicking sound with her tongue, "You will go to city of Irpin. There-"

"No!" Ren screamed. I looked down at her to see what was wrong. Her skin had turned even paler, and she was completely still.

"What is it, Ren? What's wrong?" She shook her head and said,

"Nothing. Never mind." She sheepishly hid her eyes, and I looked back to Svetlana.

"Sorry, I got distracted. What did you say?"

"Yes. There is American there. He will be very happy to see you.You leave day after tomorrow. But come back tomorrow to work." The thought of meeting another American made me excited. It almost made her comment on burned children disappear. The man in the purple suit tapped on his watch.

"Well, nice to meet you, Svetlana. I look forward to seeing

you again. Can I call you Svet?" We shook hands, then she replied,

"Yes, you can. Nice to meet you too, Pey.Ton. Robinson." After we shook hands, the man in the purple suit escorted us back to the volunteer room. Before leaving, I looked at Svetlana one more time. We gave each other the same look; I wondered if she felt the same feeling.

Ren was quiet for the rest of the day. At five, we headed back to our new home before curfew. She walked slowly beside me, quiet as a mouse; it was driving me insane. Something was wrong, but she didn't want to tell me. When we passed by the abandoned zoo, I decided to say something.

"Now that we're alone, can you tell me what you're so upset about? You screamed bloody murder earlier." Ren continued to stare at the ground as she twiddled her thumbs,

"I just don't think you should go Peyty. That's all." There was something that she wasn't telling me. Ren had never acted like that. She looked as if she was afraid of something.

"Listen, I don't like it either. We just got to Kyiv, and I kinda want to rest. But there's no time for rest. I got a job to do, and it's gotta get done. I don't know what you're so afraid of in Irpin, but it doesn't matter. We'll deal with it together just as we have this whole journey. Peyton and Ren, travel buddies. Right?" Ren nodded, but her eyes didn't change. I hugged her, took her by the hand, then we continued.

With each air raid, we stopped and looked up at the sky. I wanted to show I wasn't afraid of them, so I lit a cigarette every time it went off. Ben was right, if you're going to die, die like a man. After each boom, we high-fived then walked on. After getting inside the fence, I spent another twenty minutes trying to lock it but eventually gave up. If the Russians wanted to get in, they could get in. While we walked to Max's side of the house, Ren focused on the tree then looked up at me smirking.

"Peyty, we forgot to check the tree house." She said while running towards it. I raced after her, and caught her while she was climbing up the ladder.

"No, Ren. There could be Russians up there. I'll go." I pulled out Rider, then slowly went up the ladder to enter the tree house. It was small, but it was still big enough for me to slide onto a pillow. I yelled 'it's safe', so Ren climbed up then sat across from me. We looked out the window. Despite the occasional burned home, it was beautiful. The tall green fences closed off the colorful houses, and now we could see them in all their beauty. It looked like a rainbow, just with bits of ash.

"You know, that makes three today." Ren said matter of factly.

"Whatcha mean three?! I got us here safely." Ren clicked her tongue while counting on her fingers,

"You didn't have your phone charged, you didn't check the tree house, and you didn't say goodbye to SVET." She giggled while kicking her feet.

"First off, it ain't even like that," Ren rolled her eyes, "I mean it! Second, my phone not being charged was a blessing. I'd have a bullet in my head right now if it wasn't for my stupidity. And for the tree house, well you got me there." We both looked back out the window at the sun slowly setting.

"I think you should talk to her," Ren said abruptly, "I think it would be good."

"I don't think so," I said while kicking at a chunk of wood, "Everyone close to me gets hurt, or dies. I think it's best for everyone if I just leave people alone." Ren took a few seconds to respond.

"I don't think that's true. It just seems like that." It didn't give me any confidence. I scoffed and said,

"It's okay though. As long as everyone's safe, I'll be fine."

Ren patted me on the head, then started climbing down the ladder. Before she got off the second step, she added,

"You should still go talk to her." And with a giggle she raced down the ladder before I could say anything. Once I got down and unlocked the door, I ran towards the toilet. I'd been holding it all day, and it was time for nature to take its course. The only problem was that the toilet room was so small that my long legs wouldn't fit. I yelled at Ren to go upstairs, and for once, she obeyed. After finishing and brushing my teeth, I went upstairs then changed into my night clothes. I shut the double doors to the room and put a long metal rod into the handles for a homemade lock. The only way someone would come through would be through the window, which was locked as well. We were shut in for the night, so my anxiety got a little bit better.

Even with the heat from the water heater, it was still freezing, but Damian taught me a war trick. You stuff the bottom of your sleeping bag with your day clothes to keep your feet warm and keep them warm for the morning. You also stuff your hands in your pants; now the only thing to worry about is your head. Luckily for me, my head rested on a warm pillow on the heated floor. The only thing left to do was fall asleep, which was easier said than done.

I couldn't help but think about my future. In two days, We'd be gone yet again to another city, and I'd be tasked with my first job. I thought about the American there, and I felt a little less lonely. I also thought about plan C and plan D. The thought of the horrible acts I could commit made me shiver, but I looked over at Ren, wrapped in a blanket fast asleep on the couch. I wanted to protect her and all the people of the free world, but I wasn't sure if I could go through with it. I knew that only destiny would tell.

I didn't sleep much that night. Every few minutes, I'd hear a crack in the house or a rustle of branches outside then wake up ready to fight someone. Poor Ren didn't sleep much either because of me. After the third jolt, she stopped reacting then started to groan every time I sat up. After about the 10th jolt, she started throwing Ruby at me, but it did nothing but wake me up even more. I tried to sleep until eight then decided to prepare for the day. After getting ready, I remember looking down at my phone charger before leaving; every fiber of my being told me to take it. However, I didn't think I needed it. Svetlana told me we'd leave the day after, so I didn't need any of my stuff. As we were walking towards the front door, Ren's eyes widened, then she turned around and flew up the stairs. She returned with Ruby in hand.

"Ren. We don't need her. We're just leaving for the day." Ren pouted as she stomped towards me. She pointed to my coat pocket then said,

"We're bringing Rider. Why can't we bring Ruby?" I rubbed my temple while pulling Rider from my pocket. I explained,

"Because Rider is a KNIFE. For our protection. What is Ruby going to do against the Russians?" Ren gasped. Her cheeks went red as she shouted,

"Ruby is part of the team! She's been with us before Rider! You might think she's USELESS, but I don't." She looked up at me smirking; it was a cheap shot. There was no denying that she won that argument. I groaned, then stuffed Ruby into my coat pocket. After another fight to lock the fence door, and lost, Ren and I walked back to the train station. We were working on the military net with Ben when Svetlana came up to me, tapped me on the shoulder, then said,

"Change of plans. You leave today. You leave in one hour. Good luck." We locked eyes for a moment before I replied with a short, 'Okay.' She nodded, and after another few seconds of staring at each other, she turned red, then speeded away. I instantly began to freak out. I didn't have any of my supplies, and I was about to be leaving the city for who knows how long.

"Dang Peyty, you're screwed," Ren chimed in as she tied a pink ribbon into the net, "This might be a sign not to go." I shot her a 'don't you dare' look, and she returned to the net. There wasn't anything for me to do. The walk back home was thirty minutes at best, and I didn't want to risk not being there for my ride. This was my shot to be useful, and I didn't want to miss it.

"Nothing I can do but wing it. I'll figure it out. We're going to Irpin if we like it or not." I was too excited to start my new volunteer job and meet another American. After thirty minutes, the side door opened, and a buzzed-headed man walked in. He was short, thin, and wore a blue wind-breaker. He looked to be in his forties, but the stress on his face made him look older. He approached one of the volunteers, and they pointed at me. Ren and I went to him, then he escorted us to his car without saying a word. I waved goodbye to Ben as we drove off, and just like that, I yet again took a ride from a stranger to another far-off place. I didn't even know where Irpin was; I just knew I had a job to do.

11

IRPIN

Inside was the driver, as well as a man in the passenger seat. The driver looked almost exactly like Mundungus from the Harry Potter movies, and his uncanny resemblance made me look twice to make myself believe I was awake. The passenger was a tall, skinny man with piercing blue eyes. He gave the impression that he was smart by the way he carried himself, but also kind. None of the men spoke for the entire drive; even when we stopped and the passenger got out, nobody said a word. The man entered an abandoned building while we waited for him in the car. After 15 minutes of waiting, the windbreaker man tried to talk to me, but I told him I was American. Mundungus's head swung around faster than a top and said,

"You. American?!" I nodded, then the two men began to laugh. They started talking to one another, and I knew what they were saying: 'Another crazy American.' "What. Your. Name?"

"Peyton." Mundungus knitted his eyebrows, looked at the man in the back seat, then at me,

"Pey.Ton. I, Alexander." I shook his hand then went to the man to my left and asked his name.

"I. Alexander." I smiled. They made learning their names easy. We got out of the car, smoked, took turns pissing on a tree, and waited for the other man to return. He came out with an electric saw and a burlap sack. Mundungus Alexander pointed at me while shouting excitedly that I was American, then the man shook my hand. I asked for his name, and I kid you not, he said,

"My name. Alexander." I thought they were playing a joke on me, but there was no time to question it. I nodded, then we returned to the car and drove on. Three Alexanders, a Peyton, and a Ren. When we came to a military stop, Mundungus looked at me then put a finger over his mouth. A soldier came to the window then told us to exit the vehicle. After several soldiers searched the car from top to bottom, they gave us a thumbs up, then we drove out of Kyiv.

We drove through several destroyed subdivisions; all with blown up houses, fallen power polls, and burned cars. After going through an extremely tall forest, we made our way onto a long, flat road. In every direction were trenches, craters, and mounds of dirt across the field. Just the aftermath of a clearly brutal fight. We drove on further, dodging wreckage and potholes, then came to a massive destroyed bridge. Half the bridge laid in a river below, along with destroyed cars and broken furniture. We drove onto a side bridge that was also blown up, but two long planks connected the two ends. This was where I knew Mundungus was insane. He drove a car with five people over two pieces of wood, over a 50-foot drop to a river below, and made it.

We drove through the city entrance to a driving circle. In the middle was the name, 'Irpin,' in Hollywood letters, except the letters were ripped off and only showed the skeleton. We drove on and were stopped again by soldiers, but this time, they wanted passports. I had no choice but to give them mine, and it was the same as before. He called over his fellow soldiers, they stared at me as if I were an unicorn, then they laughed. They gave me back my passport, said thank you, then let us drive on. All of the Alexander's snickered for the rest of the drive.

We stayed in the subdivisions, but the damage worsened the deeper we drove. On every block, half of the houses were destroyed, while the other half were sprayed with bullets or had scorch marks. The only thing alive were dogs walking around in packs. Mundungus stopped the car in front of a long green metal fence with a Ukrainian flag flapping in the wind. He got out, opened up the fence, then drove in.

Inside were two houses. The one closest to the gate was an old brown house with a pile of wood and scrap metal in the front yard. A paved driveway connected the brown house with a large orange house behind it. The driveway ran all the way into the orange house's underground garage. We parked then got out. As we stretched, an old man walked out of the brown house. He was dressed in a blue camouflage jumpsuit with a matching durag. He was a short, elderly man with a long gray beard. He looked to have been in his 70s, but from his raspy voice, he could have been much older. He hugged all the Alexes then stood in front of me. He asked Mundungus about me, and he said I was American. The man's eyes lit up. He chuckled, lifted his hands, and placed a firm grip on my shoulders.

"Thank you." The man said then we locked eyes. His eyes spoke louder than anything he could have said. He'd seen a lot of pain in his life. He strongly resembled my late Grandpa Joe with how he carried himself. Tough as nails, but a heart of gold. He said his name was Igor, then we shook hands. We passed a pile of wood, paint, and nails then walked into the garage. It was clear this was the meeting place. To the left were three benches surrounding a long coffee table with two men sitting down smoking. They looked up at me, and Mundungus introduced me. After 'American' was uttered, they both rose.

"Ty Americanets?" Asked the man to the left with a light chuckle. He was an elderly man with piercing blue eyes lighter than mine. He was as tall as me and wore a half-zipped green military jumpsuit with a white tank top underneath. He gave me a bright smile. We shook hands as we locked eyes. Just like Igor's, his eyes said all I needed to know. He had seen horrific things, things I couldn't even imagine, but he was still smiling through it all.

"Alex! Call. Me. Sasha." He said with a grin while pounding on his chest. Sasha is a nickname for Alexander; don't ask me how that works it just is. I nodded then turned to the next man. He was almost as tall as me and looked to be in his early thirties. He had black eyes to match his beard and wore a US Army hat. My face lit up, thinking I'd finally met the other American.

"You're American!" I shouted while pointing at his hat, "Your hat! You were in the army? My grandfather was in the army! Did you serve in Afghanistan? What are you doing here?" But the man looked at me as if I was speaking in tongues. There was silence for a few seconds before he responded.

"I. Andre. I. Ukraine." He reached out for my hand to shake it. Confused, I shook his hand. Sasha waved for me to follow him. We walked to the right and down a little pathway, passing a fluffy brown cat. Ren and I reached down swiftly and petted it, so it purred in delight. We walked up the stairs then entered the house. Inside was a tiny room of shoes. To the right was a door that led into the living room. A long sheet of cloth was spread across the room, and on the floor was a slender, older Mexican man in a cowboy hat.

"Michael! This. Peyton. American." Sasha stepped away to reveal me. Ren sat down on an open chair, picked up the brown cat, and began to pet it.

"You're American?!" I yelled while pointing at him. I was so excited that Ren called for me to calm down.

"Yeah," he said while putting down a pair of scissors and standing up grinning. "You're American, too?" We both pointed at each other, and I leaped at him for a hug.

"Yes! I'm American! You have no idea how happy I am to see you! I haven't met another American in so long! What are you doing here, man!" The rest of the Alexes slowly walked in to watch us as if we were animals in our natural habitat.

"I'm a painter. My real name is Roberto Robbins but they like to call me Michael. I think it's because of Michael Angelo, but I'm not sure. I like to go into places like these because it fuels my work. In disasters like these, there are so many emotions that you don't feel when you're safe at home in the States. What about you? What are you doing here?" I told him my journey. He understood because he was American but was still blown away like the others.

"So what is this for?" I asked while pointing at the long white fabric.

"I'm working to make a mural for the people of Irpin. I talked to the mayor, and once I'm done, it's going to hang in the town courthouse." I asked if he needed help, but he shook his head.

"Not right now, but when we get it set up, I'll come get you. None of these guys speak any English. Asking for a hammer is like asking someone to build a rocket. But I'd love to talk to you. Not every day you get to speak English here." We sat and talked for the next hour about our lives. Roberto told me about how he moved to the US from Mexico when he was 14. He spent his life working as a carpenter until he retired early. It wasn't until he was 50 that he decided to become a painter, and had been doing it for the past ten years. I didn't believe that he was 60. He looked to be forty-five on a bad day.

The rest of the Alexes left the room, and it was just us. Only the sound of Roberto cutting cloth could be heard. I looked around the room trying to make sense of where I was. Against the back wall was a light brown bed couch, the length of which stuck out several feet. Beside the window was a couch chair that was several feet long and looked to be made in the late 80s. In the middle of the room was a fireplace with several half-burnt logs outside the hatch. On top of the fireplace were several old dusty picture frames portraying a young couple on a beach several decades ago. I picked up one of the picture frames. It was of a little boy with light blonde hair and piercing blue eyes playing on a wooden horse.

"Do you know who owns this house?" I asked while putting the picture frame back in its place.

"No idea. I don't really ask that many questions. I did hear that at the beginning of the war, during the invasion, the owner had a heart attack and had to go to the hospital. But besides that, nothing. I assume that he died."

"By the way, what's with all the Alexes?" Roberto grinned, but kept his eyes focused on the sheets.

"No idea. I guess Alex is a pretty common name here. Like Liam and Noah in America. We also have a lot of Alexes at home, too." I thought of my friend Alex back home then nodded in agreement, "I'm still working on their names. I've been here a couple weeks and still don't know everyone's name."

"Welp, that sounds like a good place to start. I'll see you in a bit, Roberto. I'm gonna go make some friends." I patted him on the shoulder then started walking towards the door. Ren hopped off the chair with the cat in hand and followed.

"I'll see you later. Peter, right?" I shook my head.

"Naw. Peyton. Like Peyton Manning. Played for the Colts? Broncos?"

"Ah, yes! Peyton Manning." I patted my hand on the doorway and began tying my shoes.

"You're probably the only person in 100 miles who understands that. We Americans have to stick together." I opened up the door then heard Roberto's last comment.

"You're right Peyton. That your right." We walked into the garage to find everyone around the table smoking. I plopped down on a wooden box covered with a blanket and pulled out my phone to check my battery percentage. It was already at 70%, and I had no idea when I'd be able to charge it.

"American?" I looked up from my phone to see a cigarette inches from my face with Igor on the other side, "Smoke?" I nodded, took the cigarette, then put it between my teeth. Igor stood up, slid his way past the others, then reached into a burlap sack hanging on the wall. He pulled something out and threw it at me. It was a blue and yellow matchbox with a tiny gnome holding a pitchfork on the cover.

I took a match out and slid it along the striker to make a tiny spark, but nothing happened. I slid it along with more force and broke the stick in half. Everyone was staring at me. I held my index finger up while smiling, then everyone around the table laughed. After two more broken sticks, I figured out the right force then finally lit the stick, just for the fire to go out before reaching my cigarette.

"You're embarrassing yourself," Ren said in a musical tone.

"I know, I know." I let out a long sigh, tried again, and broke the next two sticks until I finally got it right. I looked up while taking a puff from my cigarettes to see the Ukrainians talking. Mundungus was carrying the conversation. He appeared to be telling a joke because, after each sentence, he'd raise his right hand to his head and laugh before saying the punch line. I tried to figure out what they were saying but couldn't understand anything. It all sounded like gibberish. I took my phone out then went to Google Translate. After crafting my question, I slid my phone towards the Alex on my right. I tapped him on his shoulder while pointing down at my phone.

"You told me that all of you are Alex. How do you want me to distinguish y'all? Alex 1, Alex 2? Nicknames?" Alex studied my phone then passed it to Igor, who took one look at it before passing it to the next person until it came back to me. They all looked at me, then Mundungus spoke.

"We. No. Understand." He finished with a chuckle, and we laughed. I rephrase it.

"There are many people named Alex. I am confused. What do I call you." I slid my phone to Mundungus, and it went full circle. They talked among themselves, trying to figure out what I asked, then nodded in agreement. We went around the circle and I got everyone's names- Igor, Sasha, Alexander Mundungus, Andre, Alex Bandera, and Alex 2, but we'll call him Al. Alex Bandera was the man in the windbreaker, and Al' was the smart man in the passenger seat. I know it is confusing, but it'll get easier with time. After we finished, Alex Bandera waved for my attention.

"Translate?" he asked while pretending to type on a phone. I switched the language from English to Ukrainian then slid my phone across the table. He typed out his question as Andre and Sasha guided him through it.

"What are you doing here?" He typed. For the next few minutes, I typed my response. I told everything about my journey, from my desire to defend the free world to my trip. I hit translate and slid it back to Alex Bandera, who only read halfway before giving up, then handing my phone to Andre to finish. Judging from their faces, they seemed to have understood what I said because their faces turned from joyful to those of worry and horror.

"Parents. They know? They. Agree?" Al' leaned in, his hands together, with a concerned look. I let out a light chuckle and continued to smoke my cig.

"Yes. They. Not happy. They fine though." I finished my cigarette, put the bud into the ashtray, then reached into my pocket for another.

"No," Igor commanded. He opened his carton, pulled out a cigarette, then handed it to me, "Here." I took the cigarette and stuck it between my teeth. Sasha grabbed a lighter, walked across the table, then lit my cigarette. The guys talked among themselves. I was only able to understand 'Peyton', 'Peter', and 'America' from it.

"Pey. Ton? It is." Alex Bandera looked up as if the words were written on the ceiling. He thought briefly before waving his hand at Al' to finish.

"Pey. Ton. It. Very. Different name. We. Call you. Something else?"

"Yes," I replied. He waved at Alex Bandera to finish.

"We. Call you. **Peter.** NO! We. Call you. **Peter Bandera!**" He pointed at me, then a sea of laughter filled the garage. Just like that, I gained my war name, and a lot of friends.

For the next hour, we talked through Google Translate. I went on Facebook and showed them my family. They took a liking to my dad because of his beard. I told them about my college life and of wanting to become president. They said that Ukraine would vote for me, and even though they can't vote in our elections, it still meant a lot. Alex Bandera started chanting,

"PETER BANDERA! UNITED! STATES! PRESIDENT!" Then everyone joined in, including Ren. Amid the chanting, Roberto walked in. Alex Bandera pointed at Roberto then started to chant,

"MICHAEL BANDERA!" The rest of the guys joined in unison then raised their fists in the air. Roberto calmed them down then cleared his voice to speak.

"Okay. It is time. It is time. To. Paint." He pretended his right hand was a paint brush and swooshed it from left to right. "Time. To. Build!" Using his left hand, he leaned on the microwave and pretended to bang it with an invisible hammer. We stood up and walked outside.

"How much English do they know?" I asked.

"Not a lot. Basic words. We mainly communicate by using charades. You'll get used to it." He patted me on the back then we walked towards the pile of wood and tools. I asked him what we were doing, then he explained his plan,

"I'm making a big canvas, and we're building it together. Just way bigger than the ones you buy at the stores. I've done this dozens of times." Looking down, it seemed that he'd already gotten about halfway done with it.

"What do you need me to do?" Roberto looked around at the guys carrying wood and boxes of nails. He looked at me with a grin.

"When communication fails." Igor walked into the garage and returned with a small generator the size of a toolbox. He started the generator, and it made so much noise that Putin in Moscow could have heard it. He plugged the power saw into an extension cord attached to the generator, then the work began. For the next hour, we worked on the frame, and once it was finished, we put the cloth over it and tightened it like a drum.

"Okay. Now a fresh coat." Roberto opened a can of white paint, dipped his brush in, then began brushing from side to side along the canvas. "Peter, I mean, Peyton. Grab a brush and help me." I coughed into my sleeve and picked up one of the paintbrushes.

"You can call me whatever. Doesn't really bother me. Been

called a lot of things over the years. Can you throw me some paint?" He dipped his brush into the can then splattered some close to me,

"I want to call you by your real name. Peyton is very American. Nothing to be ashamed of. It keeps us to our roots. More of a side to side stroke not up and down. Brush more like this."

After painting for a little over half an hour, the canvas was evenly white. Roberto asked me multiple times if there were any spots that needed more paint, but to me, it looked fine. I looked at Ren, who was sitting on the stacks of paint, then asked,

"Yo, what do you think? Where do you think it needs more paint?" She didn't say anything. She kept staring off into the distance.

"Um, I'm not sure. Can't go wrong with the corners." Roberto replied. He leaned down to touch up the upper left corner.

"I don't know what's going on with you, but we'll work it out tonight. Okay?" Ren nodded slightly, and I gave a quick nod then continued painting. Once Roberto said it was finished, it was time to move it. We slowly took the canvas through a broken gate and entered the neighbor's backyard. Their house looked very old, most likely built in the late 70s. It looked to have had multiple rooms built on throughout the years. To the plot of land to our right was a massive apartment complex being built, but only its frame was set up. We walked further back into their yard towards a garage, dodging stray pipes, potholes, and roofing material. Inside the garage was an old red Buick, and while the Alexes worked to get it started, Roberto and I talked while holding up the canvas.

"Why'd you want to become a painter?" I asked.

"It's not that I wanted to become one; I'm just a painter.

You can't change what you are. Took me until I was 50 to realize it. I'm happier than I've ever been. Do you paint?"

"Naw. My family are natural artists, though. I wasn't that lucky, though. My sister Carrie does wood burning on the side."

"Well, what are you good at?" It was a good question.

"I'm not really good at anything honestly," I took a cigarette out of my pocket and lit a match, "Nothing very special about me. Everyone says that I'm smart, but then I go do dumb stuff like this." I took a long puff from my cigarette and watched as the Alexes swore and banged against the car's exterior.

"What do you like to do then? Any hobbies?"

"Truth is, no, not really. I just go to school. Well, WENT to school, hung out with friends, worked. I like doing stocks, That's something. I'm not good at it, though. I like to write, but I'm pretty bad at that too. Guess if it's not obvious, I like doing crazy stupid stuff like this." I offered him a cigarette, but he refused.

"No, I don't smoke. Thank you, though. Why do you think what we're doing here is stupid?" I paused and thought about my answer.

"Because of all the pain I've caused. My friends, my family. Not to mention all the danger that comes with it, I think anyone willingly going to war is stupid."

"Are you calling me stupid?" He asked. I laughed then exhaled the smoke in my lungs.

"You're damn right I am! We're both stupid. But," I paused, then looked over at Ren playing with the cat in the distance, "If being smart means living in fear in America and letting millions of good people die, then I'll just be stupid." I turned to Roberto to see him giving me a little grin.

"You're a good person, Peyton." It left a weird feeling in my stomach. I coughed then said,

"No, I'm not a good person. Just a person trying to be good. Believe me, I wish I was back home right now, but I just can't. The guilt would have killed me long before any of these Russian bastards would have." They managed to start the car then backed it out of the garage. After we placed the canvas down, we returned to our garage and left Roberto to do his work. For the next hour, we talked and smoked as the sky slowly turned dark. Out of the darkness came a new man dressed in a black coat with a white toboggan. Everyone greeted him, so it was clear he'd been there before.

"Hello," I said, and the man sharply turned his head. I stood to put my hand out for a handshake, "I. Peyton Robinson. American." His face lit up with joy as he shouted at the rest of the guys, 'AMERICANETS!?' Which was followed by many head nods.

"I Zhanya." He reminded me of my brother Mikey by the way he carried himself. When he smiled, it lit up the whole room, and he seemed as if he could never get blue. Zhanya sat down, then Al' walked into the garage, carrying a steaming skillet that looked like a mixture of eggs, chicken, and cheese. He set it on the coffee table, and Igor picked a bag off the ground then took out cans of tuna, a loaf of bread, and a block of cheese. Alex Bandera retrieved Roberto, then we all gathered around the table.

Igor reached beside the couch and set a large bottle of wine on the table. He then grabbed several tiny cups from a bookshelf and passed them around. Igor offered me a cup, and there was no way I'd turn it down. I'd rather die than pass up a chance to drink with Ukrainians. Everyone raised their glass then shouted,

"SLAVA UKRAYINI! HAREM SLAVA!" We clinked our glasses together then began to drink. I leaned in closer to Roberto to ask,

"Do you know what the hell they just said?"

"No idea, brother." He took a swig from his cup then used his fork to scoop breakfast casserole out of the skillet. I looked around the table to see everyone was doing the same, using their other hand to catch any falling pieces. I scooped up a chunk of chicken, and it was the best I've ever had. It tasted completely different from any chicken I'd ever had, but it was a different I liked.

"I've been here a month and everything tastes better than in America. They don't even cook it differently. It's just better. I heard somewhere it's something in the soil. That's why Ukraine is the breadbasket of Europe." Roberto informed me. We finished eating then spent the next hour drinking and smoking. Roberto and I mainly talked to each other, but tried making conversation every chance we could.

About halfway through dinner, Alex Bandera reached into his bag, pulled out a San Francisco 49ers hat, then placed it on his head. He gave me a thumbs-up, and I smiled. I'd learn a bit later why he did that. To show support for America, the Ukrainian people wear American products. It's a way to show their respect to us, give a finger to Putin, and give a little money back to America for the billions we sent. I asked Roberto where I could charge my phone, but he sighed.

"Because of the damage done to the city, we don't have electricity or running water. We barely have signal out here." The reality was settling in.

"How do we charge our phones then?"

"They have a generator that runs once a day. About five o'clock. It runs off gasoline, so they can't run it long. If you miss it, you miss it." I remembered earlier how the generator was running and everyone used it to charge their phones. I slapped my head in disappointment, then Ren laughed. I unlocked my phone and stared at the 30% power symbol. I didn't have much power, so I used the little left to explain my situation on Snapchat.

"So I assume dinner was cooked over a fire?" Roberto shook his head while taking another bite of bread with tuna and cheese, "How do we use the restroom then?" Roberto gave me a devious smile.

"Outhouse."

"I love outhouses. Way more peaceful that way. Closer to nature, too." I finished my cup of wine, then Igor immediately refilled it. I thanked him, then he said,

"No. Problem. American. Friend." He followed it with a smile covered by his bushy mustache. I stared at his and Sasha's military outfits. I typed my question, then handed it to Igor.

"You. And Sasha wear military outfit. Are you veterans?" Igor tried to read my question, but gave it to Al' to explain. Al's eyes were cold while he explained what I asked. The room went quiet as Igor and Sasha looked at each other. Sasha put his hands together, looked at me with a straight face, then said,

"We. Afghanistan war." My mind went towards 9/11. *They fought alongside Damian.* I concluded, then walked over to them. They stood, and we locked eyes. I put my hand out for a handshake.

"Thank you. For your service." Sasha and Igor looked at me in disbelief as I shook each of their hands. I wouldn't understand what I just did for a long time. After returning to my seat, I remembered the most important rule for traveling. I'd been in such a rush I'd forgotten.

"Alex?" The heads all turned to me, "I need. To learn. Ukrainian. Language. I in. Your country. I stay while. I must learn. Please. Teach me?" The council of Alexes conversed and they ended it with laughter.

"Yes. Tak." For the rest of dinner, the guys tried to teach

me Ukrainian. I'd barely gotten past the words for chair and fork when Sasha shouted, 'Peter!' as he walked out of the garage. He put his hands together to his right ear and began to snore. Roberto and I followed Sasha to the living room. Al' was propped up against the back of the bed chair while watching his phone. On the far right of the bed couch was Igor sitting on the edge, looking out the window as quiet as a mouse.

"Tam," Sasha pointed towards the bed couch. I nodded and sat down in the middle beside Igor. Roberto crawled onto my right then propped himself along the back. Sasha went to the fireplace, shoved in several logs, squirted fuel all over them, then flung a match on the pile. A fire erupted inches from his smiling face. The fire warmed the room immediately, and we began to sweat intensely. It beat the cold, though.

"DA!" Sasha turned to Roberto and I, "Good. Night." He turned around, did a joyful walk out of the room, then walked up a flight of stairs. I took off my boots and stripped down to my underwear. Igor went completely nude, snuggled under his blanket, then immediately went to sleep.

"I guess we're roommates then," I whispered to Roberto.

"Hey brother, it's an experience. You're here for it; you got it." I rested my head on a pillow then put my watch near my head. I flung a heavy hand-knitted blanket over myself and shut my eyes. I laid in a daze at everything I'd experienced in the past few hours. I was too excited to sleep.

I tried to take my mind off of everything, so I thought about my time back in college. Memories of Post seeped into my imagination as if someone poured it in themselves. I was still mad at her, but couldn't help wanting to see her again. My mind then went to my father. I remembered the night of my junior prom, I didn't get home till one in the morning. My father was in his recliner waiting for me. Once I walked in he said, 'Good, you're home,' then went straight to bed. I felt guilty while imagining my Dad in his recliner, staring at the ceiling, waiting for me to come home.

Out of nowhere, the sound of a sleeping grizzly bear echoed throughout the room. I sat up quickly. After a few seconds, the sound returned, originating from Igor. I laid back down then turned towards Roberto in an attempt to ignore Igor's snores. Roberto let out a medium-pitched snore that was followed by a long whistle. I stared at the ceiling and listened to the orchestra around me. It was as if Igor and Roberto planned it, because the other began as soon as the other ended.

The room was so hot now that just lying there without a blanket was making me sweat. All the snoring and sweating was getting to me, so I put on my shirt and pants then tip toed outside. It was freezing, but with my steaming body, it felt like heaven. I looked to my left to see Ren looking up at the moon on a wooden bench. I was so caught up with my new friends I'd forgotten to check on her.

"Hey! I'm sorry that I forgot to talk. Let's talk. What's going on?" She didn't lose her focus on the moon. I sat next to her and looked up with her.

"Peyty, when the war is over, what'll happen then?" She asked. It was something I hadn't thought too much about.

"I don't know. I figured that when I stepped into that airport, I'd never see my home again. I don't think I'll survive the war. Not with what I have planned," I laughed then looked over. She had tears in her eyes but didn't make a sound, "What's wrong, Ren?" She wiped her tears away then said,

"You don't think about yourself. Always someone else. What about you, Peyty? Why aren't you important? You're important to me." She began to sob.

"You're important to me too. That's why I'm doing this.

You matter more to me than my own life. You and the rest of the free world. Everyone back home was right. In the grand scheme of things, I'm nothing. If it means keeping you and everyone else safe, then my life doesn't mean anything." Ren stood in front of me, then yelled,

"What if you can't save anyone, Peyty?! I don't want you to be sad. I wanna keep traveling with you forever. I don't want this to end." I smiled then said,

"I don't know what I'll do when this is over. I haven't thought that far ahead. All I do know is that I like traveling with you. These past few weeks have been the craziest weeks of my life, but I wouldn't trade it for the world. Whatever the future holds, we'll deal with it together, promise." Ren fell into my arms and continued to sob. I comforted her for the next few minutes, but she never told me what was really wrong. All I could think about was keeping her safe no matter what. I went back inside, laid beside Roberto, and I slowly drifted off into a deep sleep.

12

DIG

The first thing I did the next morning was take care of business. I went through a wooden fence then ventured into a tiny forest. In the middle was the outhouse- a small straw and wood building covered in dead vines. It was everything that I ever wanted. After getting done, I took a long look in the mirror. It was hard to believe that just two weeks ago I was in Tennessee, taking tests in college, and now I was in a war zone in the middle of Europe. *Life sure is crazy.* I was unaware of how much crazier my life was about to become. After finishing my business, I went down to the garage for breakfast. Only Igor and Al' were there. Igor sat on the bench smoking a cigarette while Al' pumped water from a large jug into a kettle pot. Ren walked in then sat alone on the couch.

"Good morning, everyone," I said while sitting down next to Ren. I elbowed her lightly, but she didn't react. She cracked a weak smile then continued to stare at one of the cats at her feet. I knew something was wrong since Ren didn't want to play with her.

"Dobre ranok." Igor and Al' said in unison. Al' realized what he said then corrected himself, "Good. Morning."

"Um. Domba rancoon?" Al' let out a light chuckle then walked out of the garage. The rest of the guys entered over the next ten minutes, each announcing 'Dobre ranok' before sitting down. No one spoke besides the good morning. All were either spacing out, looking at their phone, or smoking. Roberto and I engaged in light conversation until Al' returned with a steaming kettle pot. Sasha grabbed several coffee cups from the cabinet, handed one to each person, then moved over a black bag of coffee grounds and a tiny box of green tea.

"Peter," Al' asked while hovering over me, "Coffee. Or. Tea?"

"Coffee. Please." He scooped out one spoonful of coffee grounds into my cup, poured the scolding water in, then stirred lightly.

"Thank you." I looked down at the coffee grounds floating in my drink, "What is. Thank you. In Ukrainian?"

"Dakoo you." Al' answered.

"Jackoo, you?" Grins rose on faces for the first time that day.

"No, Peyty. It's Da-koo-you." I was happy that she was speaking again, even if it was to talk down to me.

"Dakoo you," I said confidently.

"Tak! Good job." Al' said while trying not to laugh so he didn't spill any water. Sasha placed a box of crackers, a block of caramel, and a container of cream cheese on the table for breakfast. After I ate a few crackers, Sasha made a noise as if he had forgotten something, then returned to the table with a strange item. It didn't look like anything I'd ever seen before. It looked like a block of gray cheese. Al' cut a piece then handed it to me. I was reluctant to eat it, but remembered the rule: someone gives you food, you eat it. I bit down, and the chalky texture of it crumbled in my mouth with sweetness like candy.

"This. Amazing!" I leaned back then hit my head against the wall, "What. Is. This?!" Al' picked up the block then read the label.

"Sun. Flower. Seeds." I returned for seconds and thirds of this sunflower treat, mixing it with the caramel. For those wondering what it is, it's called a Halva. It was a quarter before 8 when Alex Bandera and Zhanya came in. By now, Mundungus was the only one talking. He was telling a long, serious story. Alex Bandera and Zhanya got their drinks then gulped them down quickly. Alex Bandera waved for me to follow him. We waved goodbye to everyone then walked with them to the scrap pile. Zhanya handed me two shovels, then two to Alex Bandera. He picked up a white bag beside an old washing machine then opened the gate.

"Now. We go." Zhanya said while grabbing a shovel. Ren and I followed them out of the gate then started walking. The city was empty so we could walk on the road. We dodged snake dens of downed power lines and blown-up cars. We walked down one street with more barricades than normal and saw dozens of holes in the street. After taking a closer look, we found they weren't potholes, but were grenade explosions. As horrifying as it was to know people had died in those explosions, it was beautiful. Hundreds of tiny holes orbited the crater like planets to a sun. Scattered along the street were tiny jagged pieces of metal. They ranged in size from a grain of rice to a finger. I picked up a few pieces and studied them. It was clear that they were grenade shards because they were made of rusted iron. I stuffed a few into my pocket then ran to catch up to the group.

We walked for the next ten minutes until we arrived at what I assumed to be the town square. It was a large bricked plane with buildings all around with a large metal statue of a man holding a paintbrush in the middle. He looked like a wizard with his birds flying around him as if they were his familiars. Along the north side of the square were police cars lined up along a damaged hotel with police officers moving in and out. They were the first sign of life we saw. The building had every window destroyed with the shards of glass lying on the bushes below. On top of the building were burn marks and holes revealing the destruction inside. We walked towards the police, and my anxiety rose.

I remembered what Brian had told me about the corruption in Ukraine, and the thought of being taken behind the building and shot made me clench Rider in my pocket. Irpin was a ghost town, so there were no laws anymore. Zhanya approached a huddle of police officers, pointed behind at us, then they turned. I gave a nervous wave while debating between the bushes and the urinals as a good hiding spot. The police waved at us then talked to Zhanya for a few minutes before returning to their work.

"Now. We wait." He said once he got back. He took a pack of cigarettes out of his pocket and offered me a cig. We waited for the next thirty minutes on a park bench. Each of us tried to find something to make the time go by faster. Because my phone was almost dead, I didn't want to waste what little battery left, so I decided to cheer up Ren.

"So, would you rather fight one hundred duck-sized horses or one horse-sized duck?" Ren didn't respond. *Fine. We'll do this the hard way*, I elbowed her till she groaned then said,

"One horse-sized duck."

"Come on. Do you know how big horses are?" I argued.

"Then one hundred duck sized horses." She cracked a light smile.

"That's the right answer." I looked at Ren to see her smile fade, and her emotionless stare return. Even though it didn't do much, it felt good to see her happy again, even if it was only for a few seconds. I looked ahead at the police. Something wasn't right. *Why are we meeting with police officers to dig graves? Shouldn't we be at a graveyard? Why the town square?* A few minutes later, coming from the same way we walked, came a long yellow van. It was old, with chips of paint that had been peeled off. It came to a screeching halt in front of us. The driver got out then shook our hands.

"Yah, American. Peyton." He looked puzzled while shaking my hand then looked at Zhanya, who nodded his head. His eyes beamed with excitement. The driver turned back to me, so happy you would have thought he'd just won the lottery.

"HELLO! American! Nice. To meet. You." He paused, thinking of what English words to say, "I. Am. Igor. You. Pey. Pey. Pey-"

"Peter. Call me. Peter." The four of us stared at each other, unsure of what to say. Without my translator, I was practically mute, and everyone else was, too. He talked to the police briefly before returning to the van.

"Peter. We go now." Zhanya said. We followed Zhanya to the back of the van, then he opened the double doors. We placed our shovels and the bag into the back then piled into the front of the van. There wasn't much room, so I had to sit on top of Zhanya and Alex Bandera. The driver shifted gears then followed the police cruisers.

We slowly followed behind as we drove through the deserted city. After only a few minutes of driving, the police cars stopped, and the officers got out. Three police officers climbed through a broken part of a fence, and we followed them after getting our supplies from the van. We walked into someone's backyard. The house was cut in half, with the other half scattered throughout the yard. Window panes, wooden planks, and bricks littered the yard back to a skin-and-bones dog chained to his house.

In the middle of the yard was a cross sticking out of the ground. We all approached the cross and studied it. Written on it was something in Ukrainian, but underneath it were numbers that appeared to be dates. *18, 12, 1951 to 14,03,2022. This... is a grave.* The wheel in my head started to spin.

One police officer opened a briefcase then removed a camera and a tape measure. Another officer removed a sheet of metal from the grave then proceeded to measure its length and width. While they worked on measuring the grave, one officer went to the police car and returned with a bag of dog food. He poured half the bag into the dog's food tray. It was clear by how fast he ate that he hadn't eaten in days.

After taking the measurements, they began placing markers around the yard. One of the officers hit record on the camera, then the head police officer began making a report while pointing at the grave. When he finished, he turned to us then nodded. Zhanya reached into a bag, tossed a pair of surgery gloves to Alex Bandera and me, then we put them on quickly.

"Peter. Dig." Zhanya thrusted his shovel into the grave then lifted a large chunk of earth over his shoulder. Alex Bandera pulled the cross from the ground and pressed his shovel into the grave. I was at a loss for words.

"Welp, guess we're doing this now," I whispered to myself, then stabbed the soil with my shovel to begin digging up my first dead body. While we dug, the police watched silently as they recorded. The dirt was more like sand than dirt, and easy to tear apart. It wasn't like the thick rocky earth in Tennessee, so it made sense why Ukraine was the breadbasket of Europe. It didn't make the digging process much easier, though. The three of us dug for the next ten minutes, each working on our own section until it morphed together.

Eventually, we dug so deep our shovels couldn't reach anymore, and we were beginning to get exhausted. I looked down at the three-foot hole we'd dug, and it was then that my hatred for the six-foot rule began. We all stopped to catch our breath until Alex Bandera hopped into the grave, grabbed his shovel, then continued digging. After several more minutes of digging, he dropped his shovel, squatted down, then began brushing away at the dirt with his hands. He grabbed hold of something then pulled up with all his might to reveal someone's limp leg.

"Da." He proclaimed under his breath. Zhanya jumped into the hole, so I followed. We took hold of the man's leg, lifted it up, then it let out a loud pop. The rest of the man's body slightly lifted to show where he was buried. Half of his body had risen, but the other half was submerged. We had missed him by a foot. Zhanya and I got out of the grave and started digging again as Alex Bandera stayed in the hole. Once we outlined where his body was, we began unearthing him like archaeologists.

We discovered that he was wrapped in a wool rug, and I pulled the flaps apart to reveal his decaying body. His stomach was almost gone and left only his ribcage and paper-thin skin. His eyes had sunken into his face, and his eye sockets were now filled with dirt, along with his mouth. He released an odor I'd never smelled before; I assumed it to be the 'rotting corpse smell' everyone spoke about being so bad. In my opinion, the smell of a rotting corpse isn't that bad. It's just distinct; you just know when you smell it.

I looked down at the corpse, but wasn't grossed out. I wasn't scared, I didn't feel sick, I wasn't fazed. I was numb. *It looks so fake. It's just like in the movies.* I thought to myself. I'd only ever seen a freshly dead corpse once before. It was my great-grandmother who had recently passed away in the nursing home, but I'd never seen a rotting corpse before. I stood there, staring at the corpse, imagining how he could have died until Zhanya brought me back to reality.

"Peter. Here." He pointed at the dirty blanket and made a grabbing motion. I grabbed it with both hands, then Zhanya began counting down in english.

"Three. Two. One!" We pulled the corpse out of the hole then laid it down in the yard. I hovered over the body as I tried to catch my breath. I looked into his sunken eyes and then at Ren. She looked at me horrified. I reassured her with a thumbs up, but inside, I knew everything wasn't alright. I was way too numb. I looked back toward the body, put my hands together, then whispered,

"Sorry for disturbing you." I wasn't sure how God would feel about us digging up corpses, but I wanted to make him and the man know that I had no ill intent. I was just doing what I was told. The police moved closer, brushed the dirt off his face, then took pictures at different angles.

"Peter." Zhanya waved for me to follow him. We walked back through the crack in the fence to the van. He removed his gloves and reached into his pocket and handed me a cigarette. After lighting it, I remembered what Svetlana told me, 'Dig graves.' She meant dig UP graves. It made sense why she said burned skulls, and to take lots of pictures.

The police finished then shouted for us to come back. Zhanya grabbed a body bag from the van then laid it beside the corpse. The police nodded, then we lifted the man into the body bag as gently as possible. Zhanya zipped it close, and each of us grabbed a corner of the bag then lifted him up. I struggled to carry my part of the corpse, but I held out until we made it to the van. Zhanya climbed into the van and slid his body to the back. We retrieved our shovels then smoked another cig until the police finished.

"Is this why you didn't want me to come? This ain't noth-ing." I told Ren. She didn't respond. Once they finished, we piled back into the van and followed after the police. Just like that, my life as a grave digger had begun. Our next stop was an apartment complex. Its roof was caved in, and the sides of the building were burned off to reveal the brick beneath. Every balcony was either blown up or burned to the color of charcoal. It was as if it was a gateway to hell.

We parked the van then followed the police to the apartment's playground. Along the fence were pictures of smiling suns, flowers, and children holding hands, but it was sprayed with bullets. Along the fence was the grave we were meant to dig up. Several potted plants, rocks, and flowers surrounded it. As the police began taking measurements, I strolled around the area, trying to be as careful as possible to avoid any bombs. I browsed around the parked cars. All with broken windows and bullet holes. By one of the cars was a tiny Ukrainian flag that had fallen off one of the cars. I picked it up and kept it as a souvenir.

I walked to an old wooden bench. On the bench was a toy police car, taxi, and helicopter. Children used to play in this playground, and it was now a graveyard. Tears began to swell in my eyes at the realization. The grave, the playground, the toys. Images of children being chased down and slaughtered like dogs flooded my mind, and I felt something inside me begin to crack. Thankfully, Ren came in the nick of time.

"Peyty, it's okay. Just calm down." She whispered as she tugged on my arm, "Come over and look." We walked to the grave then looked at the cross. The person who died was born in 1964, and my anger calmed, but it didn't extinguish.

"It doesn't matter how old they were, Ren. They were still innocent. They didn't deserve to die." Ren stepped away, then we began to dig. With each chunk of dirt I threw over my head, rage built inside me as my thoughts lined up with my work. The numbing feeling was being replaced with unimaginable rage. I could feel myself slipping down a dark path that I knew I couldn't come back from. I struck the body with my shovel then snapped back to reality.

I jammed my shovel underneath the body, put weight on the edge of my shovel, then the body moved up slightly. Now that we knew we had hit the body, the rest was simple. I slid into the hole and started digging around his body. He was larger than the last one. After seeing this, Zhanya went to the van and came back with a rope. He motioned for me to move, then he hopped into the hole and tied the rope around the man's legs. We grabbed hold of the rope then counted down,

"Three. Two. One!" On one, we pulled with all our might, and the man's body slowly slid out of the hole and onto the grassy playground. We caught our breath then stood to our feet.

"I'm sorry," I said while looking down at the man. We'd just pulled a man out of the ground like a vegetable. I turned to Zhanya and Alex Bandera, who had sorrowful looks on their faces. The police stared at the corpse as Zhanya fumbled to untie the rope. I looked at the man's face and saw a bullet hole slightly above his right eyebrow. The police examined the body, taking measurements of the size of the bullet hole before flipping him on his back to show the exit point. We stayed several feet back and smoked as they worked. Once they were done, Zhanya went to zip up the bag, so I dropped the Ukrainian flag in. He deserved the flag more than I did. We loaded him into the van then drove on.

We drove for a while; this time, Alex Bandera was sitting on top of us. He was the smallest of us, so it just made sense. The driver could tell that our mood was declining, so he turned on the radio and switched it to the English channel for me. The English music they were playing was very interesting. Instead of normal English songs, the songs were slowed down and mixed with dubstep. Older songs such as

'Somebody That I Used to Know' and 'Starships' were a few that played constantly. The DJ, who you would assume to speak English, spoke in Ukrainian during commercial breaks. Periodically, the DJ would change it to advertisements, and I would try to make out what they were saying from the few English words said. I could figure out the car commercials because the speaker would stop speaking Ukrainian and suddenly yell, 'FORD!'

While we drove to the next grave, I looked at the stray dogs and cats around the street. On almost every block were packs of dogs waiting on the curve. Each looked as if they hadn't eaten in weeks. We turned down a dusty road with several potholes. There were attempts to fill them. Some had thick wood covering them, while others were filled with gravel. We parked on the side of the road then grabbed our shovels. We walked down a sidewalk covered in several inches of dirt until we caught up with the police. I coughed into my elbow several times then looked to where the police were scoping around. It looked like someone was building a tomb out of white bricks but stopped a quarter of the way done. Zhanya and Alex Bandera took out a cigarette, meaning this was the next grave.

The police set markers at different objects then began the recording. The head officer stood in front of the tomb and read a long statement from his clipboard before reading off what I presumed to be a list of names. He finished then motioned for us to begin. Unlike the past two graves, this one was thick dirt with clumps of rocks. At one point, I struck something hard and reached down to find a large whiskey bottle. After twenty minutes, we had yet to find the body. The dirt was getting harder to move. Each shovel full of dirt started to feel like four.

We dug until Alex Bandera found his right foot. He let out a joyful cry, then we swarmed around the foot to realize we had been digging in the wrong direction. Alex Bandera shook the man's foot and pointed straight at the 6 feet of dirt we still needed to dig. I'd only been digging for a few hours and was already sick of it. Instead of starting from the top, we began digging a tunnel to reach his body; however, after several avalanches fell on us, we started to do it the less lazy way. The best thing about digging is it requires little communication. If I was doing something wrong, Zhanya would say, 'Peter. No. Like. This.' so I would correct myself.

Still, it had its challenges. Once we finally dug his body up, Alex Bandera turned to me and started speaking, forgetting that I didn't understand anything he said. I shook my head, and his face turned red. He started speaking much slower in Ukrainian, but it did nothing.

"I have. No. Idea. What you say." Zhanya and Alex Bandera looked at each other with a straight face. Zhanya grabbed hold of the corpse's right arm.

"Here." He held out the man's arm for me to grab. I grabbed his right arm, Zhanya his left, and Alex Bandera got his legs. We lifted him as high as we could, but the hole was so deep that we couldn't make it. We took a second to catch our breath, and we all grunted as we tried to lift him up again. We pressed his body against the walls of the hole, and I got a new grip on his back as a police officer grabbed his right arm. With both my arms pushing against his back, we managed to get him out of the hole, and he rolled over onto his back before stopping at the feet of the police officers. I said my apology to the corpse then went for my smoke break.

I was in a daze. It felt like I was outside my body, looking down on everything going on. I tried to ground myself by looking at my phone, but it was almost dead. I'd been so occupied digging up corpses that I forgot about it. I remembered that Mundungus had an iPhone, but given all the crap

I'd been through, I wouldn't have been surprised if the generator broke down the second we got back. Ren came over to
the van to stand beside me. I coughed into my armpit then
asked,

"If digging corpses ain't the reason you didn't want us to
go to Irpin, then what's the reason?" Ren didn't say anything.
She only wrapped her arms around me. I patted her on the
head then left to finish the job. We put the man inside a body
bag then carried him to the van. In the time we were gone,
over thirty people appeared out of nowhere with brooms in
their hands and bags tied around their waist. They swept the
street, moving the dirt to the sidewalk where others were
bent down, scooping it into their bags. My mood lifted
slightly. *Ukrainians don't give up. They just **keep moving
forward**. Someone blows up their house, they just sweep it away.*
We loaded into the van, then drove on to our next
destination.

13

HOUSE 43

We passed by two blue tick hounds sitting on the corner of the street, then drove a few more yards before stopping. We hopped out of the van then looked at our next destination. It was an antique house, guarded by a green fence with several bullet holes, making it look like Swiss cheese. The clouds had rolled in, making the already cold, wet, and dreary day worse. The police knocked politely, but nobody answered. They pounded on the door, then waited as someone from inside fiddled with the lock.

The door swung open, then a middle-aged man with a scruffy beard gave a quick hello before backing up. The police scoped the area for bombs before motioning for us to enter. Zhanya and Alex Bandera entered first, and I was closely behind them. Before I could cross through the gate, someone tugged on my arm. I looked behind to see Ren, snot running from her nose, screaming,

"Don't go in, Peyty! Don't do it!" Time had stopped, and it was just Ren and me.

"Ren, just tell me what's wrong. Is this why you didn't

want us to come here?" I looked over at the rusty number on the fence. House 43 was what Ren was avoiding this entire time.

"I can't tell you, but Peyty don't go in! Let's just leave. We can go anywhere, just not in there. Please Peyty. Please!" She pulled on my arm with all her might as tears flowed down her face. I looked forward at everyone inside waiting for me.

"Ren, I don't know what it is that you don't want me to see in there, but I have to. I have a job to do, but it isn't just that. I can feel it, Ren. Inside there is the reason that I came all the way here. I can't turn away now. Ren, whatever it is inside, we'll face it together." Ren shook her head.

"No Peyty. You don't understand." I plied her hands off of mine then shoved her away.

"You're right. I don't understand, because you won't tell me! I have no idea what's going on, but I will soon. Once I'm done, we're gonna talk. I don't care what it is." Ren fell on her knees and sobbed as I entered the property. The grass was overgrown, with bricks and shards of glass scattered along the yard. In the middle was an old broken birdbath turned on its side. In the corner of the yard was a grave with flowers stacked as high as its cross. The grave was smaller than the previous ones, but other than its size, it was just like the rest. The police began making measurements after placing markers around the yard at different objects. After they finished, they began recording in front of the grave. I looked over at the homeowner. He stood near the front door, arms crossed, with a look of despair.

They gave us the okay, so we began digging. I grabbed the cross at its base then pulled it from the ground without bothering to look at what was written. Zhanya carefully moved the flowers to the side, struck the dirt with his shovel, then paused. He looked down at the grave, took a deep breath, then started to dig. Much like the last grave, this one was entirely dirt, making each clump of earth we threw over our heads feel like bricks after a minute. Soon, we were several feet deep, and a black cloth was finally visible.

"Tam." I said while nudging the corner of the cloth. We continued digging around it until the corpse was entirely uncovered. Now that all the dirt was removed, Zhanya reached down, his hand trembling, then grabbed hold of one of the corners. He quickly flipped the cloth over to show the corpse of a child. A little girl of about eight in a white dress with long brown hair. Her once blue eyes had turned into dirty, hollow sockets. Reality paused again, and it was just me who could move. I fell on my knees and looked down at Ren's corpse. I climbed into the hole and moved her body from side to side. Right between her eyes was a bullet hole. I couldn't believe what I was seeing. Just a few minutes before, I was talking to her, and now she was dead in my arms.

I flipped her over and saw her back. Part of her dress was ripped off to reveal bruises and scratches along with rope burns. The Russians had tied her down to use her as their play toy before putting her down like a mad dog. Memories of our time together rushed over me like a movie. From every laugh, to every cry, to every time I carried her on my shoulders. The movie rewinded to the morning I first saw her. I remembered the nightmare before we met.

It was then I realized it all. The reason why only I could see her, the reason she didn't want me to go to Irpin, the reason she came to me after the nightmare. She was a ghost, and God had sent her to push me to go to Ukraine just to dig her up. That was the destiny he planned for me. He wanted me to look Ren in the face, and know that I was too late. Something inside me cracked. I pulled her lifeless corpse into my arms and begged her to wake up, but no amount of wishing would bring her back.

I cried seemingly for hours as I held her, wondering why

she had to die. Why couldn't it have been me instead? So much rage was inside me I wailed with all my might. Out of all the people on Earth that God could have chose, he chose me. Out of 8 billion people, I got the golden ticket to the factory from hell. Why was this my destiny? Why was this the path that I had to follow? Why, God, do I have to suffer? Why did Ren have to die for a useless piece of trash like me? What's the lesson? As if it was all a dream, reality restarted, and I was outside the hole. Zhanya hovered over Ren as we all looked in awe. Zhanya regained his composure, grabbed Ren's right arm, then looked at me.

"Peter?" I stepped into the hole and grabbed her left arm, while Alex Bandera got her legs. We picked her up then started to climb out of the hole when she started making a gurgling noise. I looked down at her to hear the sound growing louder and louder from her mouth. With every step we took, the gurgling sound changed. Blood gushed out of her mouth while flowing down her face onto my boots. It was as if she was trying to speak. All I could hear was her asking me for help, but it was too late. My entire body began to tremble, and my grip on her was loosening. Zhanya noticed and said,

"Peter. It. Okay." But it wasn't okay. I used every ounce of willpower and carried her out of the hole then onto the green grass. We stood in silence as we stared at the rotting corpse of a child. Those are words I never thought I'd say; words that nobody should ever have to say. Once the police began working, Zhanya and Alex Bandera silently walked towards the van. Alex Bandera climbed into the van, and slammed the door behind him. Zhanya walked to the front of the van, took out a cigarette, then looked out into the empty street. I went to Ren's cross. After translating, it read, '*Renova Babich, October 10, 2013-March 15, 2022. I could've saved her if I left when I should have. I could've saved all of those people rotting away in the back of our van.* I went up to Ren's father. He looked at me with tears flowing down his face. His eyes were the same piercing blue as Ren's.

"I'm sorry," I said to her father. He looked at me, confused, but he pulled me in. We hugged for a moment before I pulled away. I didn't want him to see me cry. I went to Zhanya then asked,

"Zhanya. That. Child?" I had to be sure it wasn't all in my head. Zhanya didn't say a word. He only smiled, his eyes watering, while nodding his head. I stood there, unsure of what to say. I nodded, then walked to the back of the van. My body was trembling; my heart felt like it was about to burst out of my chest. I looked down at my boots, then at my gloves. I was covered in her blood. I took my gloves off frantically then threw them in a bag on the sidewalk.

"This is bullshit. This whole thing is bullshit!!!" I yelled as I beat against the van. I slapped my wrist with the rubber band until it snapped off. The blue tick hounds from down the street started prancing towards me from all the noise I was making. Tears began to build in my eyes, but I wasn't strong enough to stop them from flowing.

"I failed... I couldn't save her. I let her down. I let everyone down. She's dead because of me. Why God?! Why is this happening? WHAT'S THE LESSON!?" The dogs moved closer then licked my hands hanging off the van. I petted them to find some form of comfort. One of the dogs turned his head sharply and looked towards the plastic bag.

He pranced over to the bag, dug through it, then slowly returned to me with something in his mouth. He stuck his head out towards my hands to show what was between his teeth. It was my gloves. The second dog dropped to the ground then began licking my boots clean. I sat completely still, not a thought in my mind, as I stared at the dogs. Something snapped. All the darkness inside me poured out. I rocked back and forth, unable to control my laughter and sobbing.

"She's gone, and she's never coming back. If I wasn't such a coward and left when I knew I should have, then maybe I could have saved her. Maybe I could have saved all of them. This is my punishment, God. This is truly hell. I understand why you brought me here. It was to tell me what needed to be done. That's the lesson. It doesn't matter what I want, it doesn't matter what I feel. I can't afford to be Peyton Robinson, the world can't afford it. I have to be Peter. I have to wipe them all out. All of our enemies. It doesn't matter if they're innocent or not. **It doesn't matter when you die because everyone dies eventually**. I'll do what I must to stop Him. As long as my people are safe, I'll be the boogeyman. I won't let any more of my people die." I reached into my pocket then pulled out our Lady Liberty key chain. I was holding onto it for Ren, but she didn't need it anymore. No ounce of happiness was inside me anymore. I was truly alone, and all I could feel was darkness.

I reached for my gloves, but the dog held them tightly. We started having a tug of war for the gloves, but he wouldn't give up an inch. I took a deep breath, gently patted his head with one hand, and pulled slightly on the gloves with the other. The dog released his grip, and the gloves were mine once again. I looked down at the gloves then up again. Ren was lying in front of me, but she wasn't the Ren I knew. Her skin was gray and folding; her eyes were sunken into her thin skull. The hair on her head was balding with what little left was long and frail. She reached her hand out towards me while trying to speak, but nothing besides gurgling sounds and blood came out. I couldn't bare to look at her.

Zhanya appeared then nudged his head towards the

house. We walked back while I put my gloves back on. We lowered her into a body bag. As Zhanya began zipping up the bag, I gave one last look at her, *I'm sorry Ren.* Zhanya zipped the line across her face. She was now just another corpse for us to move to the van; the only difference was this one was lighter.

After carrying her to the van, we crammed in, then the driver took off. Still in shock, I didn't notice that we didn't wait for the police. We drove for over thirty minutes in silence before I snapped back to reality. We turned left then came to a complete halt atop a hill, looking down at the multi-lane road. Many of the lanes were blocked off by sandbags and metal jacks, but also by blown-up tanks with the letter 'Z' painted along their sides. Hanging off the trunk of the tanks were Ukrainian flags flapping in the wind; some burned, some torn, but all were flying.

I looked down the hill, then realized why we had stopped. Dozens of soldiers were scattered along the road, standing at attention. Two soldiers walked up to our van then asked for passports. Igor pointed to us, covered in dirt and blood, then at a sticker stuck to the bottom left windshield with a number and the word 'Volunteer.' The soldier nodded, walked to the back of the van, opened the doors, then returned to us with a serious look. He gave us the okay, and we carried on.

We reached the bottom of the hill where the soldiers had made a sandbag base. They let us pass through, but not without nervous stares. After a little more driving, we arrived at our destination. Before entering the building's parking lot, I knew what we were there for because of the smell of rotting corpses. There were several yellow vans parked outside of a big, bricked building. Beside it was a long 18-wheeler trailer with several people in hazmat suits standing in front of the door. We drove up to the trailer, then

Igor pointed at the number. The hazmat people unlocked the trailer and opened the doors, then we backed the van up to it.

I got out of the van, then walked to the trailer to look inside. It was filled with hundreds of body bags stacked on top of each other. Not wanting to appear weak, I climbed into the trailer. Zhanya and Alex Bandera lifted the first corpse into the air, so I grabbed it then slid it into the trailer. It was Ren. Zhanya motioned for me to go back, so I slid her body further into the trailer. Zhanya climbed in, grabbed hold of her, and we lifted her onto a stack of three other people.

I apologized while staring at the floor. One of the body bags was ripped open, and a green moldy hand was sticking out as if he was trying to bring me to the afterlife with him. Near the entrance was a small dark green coffin, the size of a toddler, sitting on top of an adult-sized one. We did the same for the second and third body. On the fourth body, we tried lifting it, but the tower of corpses was so high now that we couldn't lift it high enough, and the corpses crashed onto my feet. Including Ren's.

I kept my cool, and we tried again. This time, we placed them on a shorter stack. I jumped off the trailer, took off my gloves, then tossed them in a trash can. One of the hazmat suit men squirted hand sanitizer into our hands and told us good job. I gave one last look into the trailer at her body bag. I wanted her to unzip it then come running into my arms, yelling, 'It was just a prank, Peyty.' But I knew that was impossible. Ren was dead, and no amount of wishing would bring her back. The trailer doors closed, and she was gone.

The driver brought us home, or as I liked to call it, 'Irpin Homebase.' We placed our shovels down where we gathered them that morning then walked into the garage to find Sasha and Andre sitting around the table. Sasha seemed to be telling a funny story because Andre was laughing behind his phone. Upon seeing us, Sasha stood up. He shook each of our hands, and when he came to me, he said,

"Hello. My. Friend." With a smile. I wasn't in the mood to speak, but I knew that I had to keep up my appearance. I couldn't let them see how upset I was no matter what. I put on a fake smile.

"Hello! Ukrainian friend! Smoke?" I pulled a carton of cigarettes out of my shoulder pocket then opened it. He let out a long 'oh' while plucking one out. Alex Bandera seemed to be talking about our day, because of the occasional shocked expressions from Andre and Sasha. The entire time they conversed, I kept a grin on my face, but on the inside, I was spiraling. I couldn't get Ren's decaying corpse out of my head.

The generator started shortly later, then Igor shouted it was ready. My phone was sitting at just 2%. I had just enough to ask Mundungus for his spare charger. I typed my question then handed him my phone. He grinned while motioning for me to follow him. We walked to the neighbors yard to an old black 80's Buick. He reached inside then handed me his spare.

"Jakoo you JAKOO YOU!" I replied happily. We walked back to the generator, then I plugged in my phone. I took a second look at my phone as I stood up. It wasn't charging. I was about to have another breakdown. I fiddled with the charger, moving the tip side to side, but nothing changed. Applying more force, I thrusted the charging tip further inside, then the percentage bar turned green. I wrapped the wire around my phone, set it down slowly, then lifted my hands as if there was a gun to my face. I stared at my phone, waiting for the green to fade back to black, but it didn't. It was a much-needed win.

"Where. Roberto?" I asked. Andre looked up from his phone, and he made brushing strokes in the air with his left hand. I walked to the neighbor's garage. Roberto was working on the right side of the canvas, painting a long blue strip at an angle. He stood back, studied it while tapping his chin with his paintbrush, then rushed to the left and painted a circle. He wore a black cowboy hat and a bullet belt wrapped around his shoulder like a sash, but instead of bullets, he had paintbrushes. I watched him as he worked for a few minutes, but he seemed not to notice me. His painting was random, mainly shapes and lines going in every direction. After finishing a rigid rectangle, he turned around then jumped.

"Oh, Peyton. I didn't see you there." He put his paintbrush into one of his holdings then sat down on a stool. "How was your day?" Ren's decaying face swept across my mind, as did the image of me tossing her into the trailer like a sack of potatoes.

"It was alright. Your painting is coming along pretty well. But, um, what are you trying to do?" I lit my cigarette, as we both studied the canvas.

"I'm not so sure myself. I kind of work my way into it. It just comes to me as I go." He replied.

"It looks very abstract, but it looks pretty cool." We both continued staring at the painting, unsure what to say. I've never been good at making small talk. Especially when I'm having a bad day. I'm more of a random conversation type of guy; only once I've gotten to know someone can I communicate. However, we both had the same understanding. It didn't matter if we liked each other or had anything in common; the only way we could talk was to each other.

"So, what did you do today?" He asked.

"Well," I took a long puff to avoid the conversation, "We dug up bodies." I gave him a heartfelt smile. His eyes widened, and his body tensed.

"Like, from graves?" Roberto put his hands on his hips then moved his head from side to side.

"Yeah. We dug up graves with the police supervising us. They also took records of everything." There was a long pause. The birds chirping outside was the only noise.

"That must have been hard. You okay?" I smiled with my hands behind my head.

"Oh yeah, I'm good. It wasn't that bad. You know, they say the smell of rotting corpses smells awful, but honestly, it's not that bad. It's just a distinct smell. Kind of like rotting meat mixed with rotting vegetables and freshly cut grass." While I talked, my cigarette burned down to the filter, so I flicked it away. I didn't want to leave immediately to show how upset I was, so I tried to make more conversation.

"So you speak Spanish? I took Spanish in high school, but I've forgotten most of it. It didn't help that our teacher was crazy. My brother Mikey had her years before and told me that she would put mirrors on the wall to watch the students as they took tests. But by the time I got there she stopped. I guess someone finally told her it was crazy! You said you came to America when you were 14. did you already know English? Did you have to go to school?"

"I knew some, but it didn't take long to pick up English. For school, no, but I made it work." I paced around the canvas, trying to find something to say, but there isn't much you can discuss about a square.

"Was it hard learning English? Spanish and English are pretty similar, but all the slang makes it almost impossible." I lit another cigarette to keep my hands from fidgeting, "I doubt I'll ever understand whatever the hell those guys are saying." Roberto let out a light chuckle that made some awkwardness disappear, "Alright, Roberto, I don't want to take away from your painting. I'll see you at dinner." I started walking towards the house, but he tapped me on my arm and said,

"If you ever want to talk about it, I'll listen. I know it must have been hard." He nodded, and I removed my cigarette from my lips to say,

"I appreciate it, Roberto, but I'm fine. Thank you though." He nodded again while taking out a brush then strutted towards the mural. Time seemed to have been moving at a third of the pace. I needed some time alone, so I went to the house to lay on the couch. I stared at the ceiling, lost in my mind about what transpired. I curled into a ball and clung tightly to Ruby. She was missing her too.

The image of Ren's corpse wouldn't leave my mind. I tried thinking of something else, anything else, but every time I pictured my friends and family, they would turn into rotting corpses with blood gushing out of their mouths as they turned towards me. If I wasn't fixated on the dead, I was thinking about my meltdown. My rage was so powerful it felt as if it was going to burst out of my skin. The dark thoughts of what I'd do, of what my plan was. It felt as if I'd fallen into a dark canyon. I tried to grasp at the walls to stop myself from falling any further, but I couldn't.

The room got darker, and the ceiling started to sway. I stopped trying to hold onto the canyon walls. It was pointless. The images of Ren's corpse made me sink so far that the couch seemed to transform into a rocky, cold surface with jagged spikes poking into my pores. I felt like I was going to make the house explode, just like what the Russians did to so many there. I faded into that darkness until I sat up quickly, desperate for air, then stared straight ahead at the clock.

Its constant ticking made me start to go insane. I had to go somewhere quiet. I walked outside then went to the out house. I sat down on the toilet, then looked at myself in the mirror. There was someone else looking back. Someone who looked just like me, but different. Almost as if my reflection was from another dimension. I glared at my reflection.

I'm just trippin. There's no way. I thought while leaning in closer. My face was so close to the mirror that my breath was beginning to produce a fog. It was me, but I looked older. Not from my wrinkles, but from my eyes. It's hard to even put into words, but my eyes had changed. I knew what it was. I'd heard about it, but didn't know it could happen so soon-I'd gotten my thousand yard stare. My 'Sharingan' as I call it. My eyes no longer showed a bright eyed cheerful person, but someone who was broken and hurting. I closed my eyes for a moment, then opened them hoping I was imagining it. But I wasn't. Those same eyes were staring back at me.

I wanted to cry, not because of Ren, but from what it meant. I'd known from the start that war would change me, but now I knew for sure it had. I had changed, and there's no way to go back. I knew that I wasn't a kid anymore. I was an adult. My childhood was officially over. The proof was in my eyes, and in my soul. I wasn't that good hearted kid that left America, wanting to save a little girl. I was a broken man, filled with the will to destroy. Willing to kill innocents for the sake of his people. I was without a shadow of a doubt now, the same inside and out as him. *We're the same. I have the same eyes as you, Putin.*

I stumbled to my feet then went to go join the rest in the garage. I tried to converse with everyone, but without a translator, it was nearly impossible. I wasn't sure what to talk about, so I went with things I loved.

"Football. Yah like football." I drew a football on a piece of paper as everyone looked down to see. They gave me nods of understanding, letting me know to keep going. "In Tennessee. We. Titans!" I beat on my chest and made a loud Yi-Yi, "But we lose. A Lot." We talked until Al' served dinner.

He served us a popular Ukrainian red soup called borsch. Igor went around the table and filled everyone's cups with wine. After everyone was served, Sasha raised his glass into the freezing garage air, and we all clinked our cups while shouting, 'Slava Ukrayini! Harem Slava!' After downing my cup, I leaned in close to Al'.

"What does. Slava Ukrayini! Harem Slava! Mean?" I had to repeat myself three times for him to understand. He typed his response on his phone,

"It means- For the glory of Ukraine! For the glory of the heroes!" I nodded in understanding. I thought how that chant would never apply to me. I looked down to see that my glass had magically refilled. As I drank, I realized the wine tasted better than the night before. We dived into our dinner like a pack of hungry lions. I looked around the table to see everyone pouring a white sauce into their bowl and on their bread. I squeezed the sauce onto my bread and dipped it into my bowl then took a bite. The sauce was mayo, the best mayo I've ever tasted in my life. I'd never been the biggest fan of mayo, but this mayo seemed to have been sent from heaven. I squeezed a few lines into my bowl then took a spoon full.

"Holy crap!" Everyone looked up from their bowls confused, "Um. Soup. Good!" I gave a thumbs up, then they continued with their meal. Halfway through dinner, Roberto stumbled into the garage then sat down beside me.

"Evening, Roberto. How's the painting going?" Roberto thanked Al', who had handed him a bowl, then took a swig of his wine.

"Pretty good. Got a good base. Ah, borsch night!" After we finished, the sun had completely set, making the bulb hanging from the ceiling the main source of light. Roberto and I conversed about our lives, telling stories of the craziest stuff we had done. The guys were watching us curiously; I assumed they were playing the English game. After slapping my hand on my knee, I finished my fourth cup of wine. The image of Ren's pale corpse didn't seem to bother me as much. Joy started to fill my mind from the tingling over my body. For the first time all day, I didn't have to fake a smile. It was stuck on my face as if someone had used a hammer to drive nails into my dimples. After dinner, Zhanya and Mundungus brought me over to the abandoned building's back porch. Mundungus pulled out a bottle of crown hidden underneath a workbench.

"Yes. Please." I said as he poured me a cup. We took shot after shot until we couldn't stand anymore. With every shot, happiness grew inside me. After shot number five, he pulled out a homemade gravity bong, seemingly out of nowhere, and filled it with tobacco and marijuana. I'd never smoked out of a homemade gravity bong, but I was drunk enough to try. I inhaled a bottle's worth, and once I released the smoke, I lost all feeling in my legs. I fell down on the steps then pointed towards the sky at the millions of bright dots shining down on me. *Maybe I'm just overthinking everything. Maybe my life isn't hell after all,* I told myself. After another hour of partying, I could feel it was time to stop.

"I. Sleep." I put my hands together then put them against my cheek and made a loud snore. They laughed while nodding their heads.

"Nadobranich." Zhanya replied.

"Um. Nato, brakich." I walked backward towards the fence then tripped over a piece of wood, and fell on my butt. I laid on the cold grass, cackling uncontrollably with everyone else. I looked up at the night sky again. Time seemed to have stopped, and it was just me. The cold blades of grass pressed against my back, and the warmth from the liquor made a weird sensation roll over me. It was one of the worst days of my life. I'd seen the corpse of my close friend earlier, and there I was, laughing and having the time of my life. I pulled Rider out of my coat pocket then reached up at the stars. Something was deeply wrong with me, but it didn't matter. I had to do whatever it took to protect the free world. I had a job to do. I had to keep moving forward. I had to rally for Ren.

To Be Continued...

Made in the USA
Monee, IL
09 February 2025

11771803R00109